THE COMPARATIVE APPROACH IN AREA STUDIES AND THE DISCIPLINES

Problems Of Teaching And Research On Asia

Selected Papers Presented at the Conference on Asian Studies
and Comparative Approaches Sponsored by the Comparative
Studies Center, Dartmouth College, September 13-17, 1965

Edited by
Ward Morehouse

Occasional Publication No. 4

Foreign Area Materials Center
University of the State of New York
State Education Department, New York, 1966

Printed in India, at Everest Press, 4 Chamelian Road, Delhi-6

Contents

Page

FOREWORD, Wing-tsit Chan, Comparative Studies Center, Dartmouth College

PREFACE, Ward Morehouse, Center for International Programs and Services, State Education Department, University of the State of New York

SOCIAL ANTHROPOLOGY AND THE COMPARATIVE STUDY OF CIVILIZATIONS, Milton Singer, University of Chicago .. 1

COMPARATIVE LITERATURE STUDIES, CRITICAL AND HISTORICAL: SOME POSSIBILITIES AND SOME LIMITS, George L. Anderson, Modern Language Association .. 14

COMPARATIVE MYTHOLOGY AS AN INTRODUCTION TO CROSS-CULTURAL STUDIES, Joseph Campbell, Sarah Lawrence College .. 22

APPROACHES IN THE STUDY OF JAPAN, Donald Shively, Harvard University .. 29

COMPARATIVE STUDIES IN UNDERGRADUATE EDUCATION, Wm. Theodore de Bary, Columbia University .. 38

A CONCEPTUAL REVIEW OF AREA AND COMPARATIVE STUDIES: SOME INITIAL REFLECTIONS, C.K. Yang, University of Pittsburgh .. 46

A NOTE ON THE FOREIGN AREA MATERIALS CENTER .. 55

SOME PUBLICATIONS OF THE FOREIGN AREA MATERIALS CENTER .. 56

APPENDIX: CONFERENCE ON ASIAN STUDIES AND COMPARATIVE APPROACHES .. 57

Foreword

Asian studies in the United States have long passed the stage of being intellectual curiosities, hidden in an obscure corner of the curriculum for a few exotic souls. In many colleges and universities they are still being pursued primarily for a utilitarian purpose—to understand current Asian problems and to train specialists for trade, diplomacy, and other fields of activity. An increasing number of institutions, however, have realized that no education is truly liberal or complete until there is opportunity for study of all significant human experience, regardless from what quarter of the earth they may come. This does not mean an encyclopaedic survey of all history in all lands but a critical examination of those meaningful events or ideas that can broaden the student's vision and enlarge his understanding of our human heritage. In other words, Asian studies must form an integral part of the curriculum.

When the several disciplines are thus broadened and enriched, Asian history and thought and those of the West will inevitably be compared and contrasted since they are vastly different. This new approach will raise many questions. Are area studies and comparative studies compatible? What is the relation of comparative studies to infusion in the curriculum, faculty development, and other programs? What can be compared within Asian studies? What is the status of the comparative studies concerning Asia in various disciplines? What areas of comparative studies are suitable for undergraduate education in so far as Asian studies are concerned? How can comparative studies be promoted in undergraduate education and in more advanced programs of training and research?

In an effort to find answers to questions like these, the comparative Studies Center of Dartmouth College held a conference on September 13-17, 1965. Thirty-six specialists from its own faculty and other institutions were invited to present papers or to comment on them. They were not asked to confine themselves to the specific questions raised above but to express whatever ideas they had and do so in any manner they chose. The purpose was to provide for a free exchange of views and to stimulate discussion.

Ten papers were presented on as many subjects. Those specifically dealing with Asian studies and comparative approaches are published here with the hope that they may prove of interest to individuals and institutions elsewhere concerned with these problems.

Papers dealing with other subjects such as studies falling entirely within one civilization or contemporary society are being published separately.

My colleagues, Professors Francis W. Gramlich and Laurence I. Radway, Co-Directors of the Center, and I are grateful to Ward Morehouse for his help in many ways in making the conference fruitful and enjoyable. We also want to thank him for the opportunity to publish these papers as one of the Foreign Area Materials Center *Occasional Publication*.

Wing-tsit Chan
Co-Director
Comparative Studies Center
Dartmouth College

June, 1966

Preface

One of the important problems confronting the social sciences and humanities today is the interrelationships between comparative and area studies and their role in turn within the academic disciplines. The complexities of these interrelationships have been underscored in recent years as the social sciences and humanities have begun to broaden the spectrum of their concerns beyond the perimeters of Western civilization. But the phenomena of comparative and area studies in American colleges and universities are not new.

Area studies have been a part of the college and university curriculum in the United States as long as we have had the classical studies of the origins of Western civilization. Indeed, classical Oriental studies—in which the organizing theme is a major historical tradition to be explored from the religious, philological, literary, and philosophical vantage point—have had a small but honorable place in American universities for over a century. But the study of contemporary, as well as historical aspects of major regions of the world beyond Europe—involving both the social science and the humanistic disciplines—is a relatively more recent development in American academic life, particularly since the Second World War.

In a similar fashion, comparative studies have been an element in the academic landscape for many decades. The motion of the pendulum has in many ways characterized the rise and fall—and now rise again—of comparative studies. The origins of the discipline of anthropology in the latter half of the nineteenth century offer some interesting parallels with the ferment characterizing that discipline—and a number of other social sciences—today.

This group of papers explores some of the problems generated by the growth of interest in area and comparative studies in programs of teaching and research in American colleges aud universities. Several of the papers reflect the increasing emphasis on rigorous analysis and correspondingly more modest claims which characterize the renaissance of comparative studies in recent years. The range is wide—from a discussion of social anthropology as an instrument of comparative analysis and the comparative possibilities in literature to consideration of the implications of such possibilities on the undergraduate curriculum. But, while the range is wide, it provides little more than a sampling of the process of stimulation and change in teaching and research in the social sciences and humanities today.

This process of fermentation and change provides the basis for about the only generalization which can safely be made about such a diverse group of papers. Whatever may be claimed for the contribution of the established disciplines to the study of foreign areas or area studies to the disciplines, this interaction is an important factor in generating the far-reaching changes now occurring in teaching and research in American higher education. And a significant element in all of these developments is the phenomenon of breaking out of the traditional boundaries of Western civilization.

This phenomenon was the underlying theme of the Conference on Asian Studies and Comparative Approaches organized by the Comparative Studies Center at Dartmouth College in September of 1965. All of the papers which appear here were first presented there.

Although this publication would have scarcely come about if the Comparative Studies Center at Dartmouth had not taken the initiative in organizing the conference, the present publication is not a report of the conference, at least in an inclusive sense. Several of the papers prepared for the conference are not included here because the particular character suggested the merit of publication elsewhere or because, while they dealt with the general theme of the conference, they were not so directly related to the interrelationship of area and comparative studies and the disciplines which is the concern of this *Occasional Publication*. Responsibility for this determination rests in the final analysis with the undersigned who bears general editorial responsibility for publication of the papers included here.

While the final responsibility has been mine, I have been aided by the editorial assistance of Hugo Jaeckel and Edith Ehrman. Responsibility for seeing the publication through the process of reproduction has been borne by Miss Ehrman, Manager of the Foreign Area Materials Center, and by Vineeta Singh of the Educational Resources Center in New Delhi.

Appreciation must be expressed to Professor Wing-tsit Chan, Co-Director of the Comparative Studies Center at Dartmouth, for his patience during the protracted period of exploring possibilities for publication and his cooperation in many other ways. And to the authors of the papers goes an equal measure of thanks for their forebearance and willingness to suffer the exercise of what in some cases has been more than the usual editorial prerogatives.

This collection of papers is being issued under the auspices of the Foreign Area Materials Center, the primary objective of which is strengthening material resources useful in teaching about foreign areas, particularly at the undergraduate level. The Center which is an adjunct of the New York State Education Department's Center for International Programs and Services, is further described at the end of this publication.

WARD MOREHOUSE
Director
Center for International Programs and Services
State Education Department
University of the State of New York

June, 1966

Social Anthropology and the Comparative Study of Civilizations

MILTON SINGER*

The Methodological Postulates of Social Anthropology

In his article on "Civilization", written for *Collier's Encyclopaedia* just before his death, Robert Redfield does not cite a single social anthropologist and only one anthropologist of any kind, A. L. Kroeber. His references are to philosophers of History—Danilevsky, Spengler, Toynbee, and others—as sources for the grand conception of the comparative study of major civilizations in their origins and development; and to the archaeologists and prehistorians who have been accumulating detailed factual knowledge on the origins of the early civilizations in the old and the new worlds. Allowing for the fact that an encyclopaedia article imposes, severe space restrictions and permits only painting the highlights of a subject, the omission of any reference to social anthropology is nonetheless significant.

Redfleld considered himself a social anthropologist, and most of his work at least during the last few years of his life, from about 1948 to 1958, is an effort to adapt the concepts and methods of social anthropology in collaboration with those of the philosophy of history, archaelogy, and history, to a comparative study of civilizations. Indeed, the conception of civilization which he sketches in the *Collier's Encyclopaedia* article, as an alternative to Gordon-Childe's ten diagnostic criteria of civilization, is itself an extended social anthropological conception. And in some of his other later writings one can find his own detailed account of how this conception grew out of and is related to the concepts and methods of social anthropology.[1]

The fact that inspite of the background of work in social anthropology, Redfield in the article did not mention a single social anthropological contribution to the comparative study of civilizations does not mean that he thought of social anthropology as incapable of making any contribution. He probably did not regard any particular contribution as sufficiently noteworthy, and also considered the changes required in social anthropological concepts and method to make them suitable for a comparative study of civilizations, sufficiently radical and controversial to raise questions in his colleague's mind whether this new kind of anthropology should still be called "social anthropology."

*Milton Singer is Paul Klapper Professor of the Social Sciences and Professor of Anthropology at the University of Chicago. He also served as Executive Secretary of Chicago's Committee on Southern Asian Studies. From 1953 to 1961, he was Associate Director of the Redfield Project on Comparative Civilizations. He is a Fellow of the American Anthropological Association.

To one familiar with presentations of social anthropology as the comparative and holistic studies of integral societies and cultures, Redfield's diffidence may appear as excessively fastidious. A closer acquaintance with theory and practice of contemporary social anthropology leads to an appreciation of his circumspection. For social anthropology cannot in fact enter seriously into a study of civilizations unless it modifies some of its underlying methodopological postulates and assumptions. What these are and in what respects they have to be modified for civilizational studies are briefly indicated in the paragraphs following.

There are three major methodological postulates which, taken together, distinguish the discipline of social anthropology as developed by Malinowski, Radcliffe-Brown, and their followers. These are postulates in the sense that they define appropriate objects of study, methods of research, and concepts and theories. As such they are not based on specific research, nor can they be confirmed or refuted by specific research. They constitute a definition of the "culture" of social anthropology, of those beliefs and practices to which anyone wishing to call himself a social anthropologist will need to adhere. In the history of anthropology as in science, they represent what Kuhn calls,"a paradigm" which has developed in dialectical reaction to a previous paradigm and will, in turn, be superseded by another paradigm.

The first methodological postulate is *populism*, the belief that the proper object of study, for social anthropology, is the everyday life, activities, and products of the common people, whether these people be primitive, preliterate, illiterate, folk, peasant, or urban. This represents a reaction to the preoccupation with activities and products of elites—literary texts, philosophy and theology, science, the fine arts, dynastic political history. In committing themselves to this postulate, social anthropologists were rejecting the "classical" approach to their own culture as well as the transplanted "classicism" of the orientalist studies of Asian civilizations.

The acceptance of this postulate among anthropologists seems to coincide with the growth of popular democracy and the philosophy of the "common man", and is probably also closely associated with the romanticization of the "folk" and the "primitive".[2] Its prevalence among American anthropologists is easily discerned, from Boas' studies of the Baffin Island Eskimo to Oscar Lewis' studies of the "culture of poverty" in New Delhi, Mexico City, San Juan, and New York.

In an article on "The Ethnological Significance of Esoteric Doctrines," Boas himself explicity defended "the necessity of knowing the habits of the thought of the common people" even as expressed in the grossest stories against those ethnologists who wanted to know only "the ideal Indian" through the study of "refined", esoteric knowledge."[3]

The fact that social anthropologists sometimes concentrate on political and cultural elites in the primitive societies they study does not contravene their populism. The notion that primitive peoples could have "culture" and an orderly social life that might be usefully compared with the culture and society of European civilization, of ancient Greece and Rome, and of oriental civilizations was precisely the way in which "the comparative method" of nineteenth century anthropology enlarged the classicist's conception of "culture" beyond the boundaries of a small corpus of literary texts and artistic monuments to include the great variety of "primitive" social and cultural forms from which the "great traditions "of civilization evolved.[4]

Such an extension of the "culture" concept is especially evident in the development of linguistics. Indo-European linguistics was created by scholars trained in the "classics" who sought to compare "Oriental classics" in Sanskrit and Avestan with Greek, Latin and other European languages. Sanskrit and Indo-European linguistics were thus incorporated into classical and Germanic studies. When the hold of the classical models in language and literarure was weakened to this extent, it remained only for more venturesome anthropologists and linguisties—a De Sassure, a Boas, a Sapir, a Bloomfield—to develop the notion of a descriptive linguists for any language whatever. It is still possible to find living linguists whose careers recapitulate this 150 years of intellectual history as they passed from classics to Sanskrit to descriptive linguistics and ethnography.

The comparative, non-normative approach to the study of culture, language, and social institutions introduced by anthropology is usually referred to in terms of a doctrine of cultural and linguistic relativity. This doctrine does not rule out the existence of universals in language and culture; it merely insists that the discovery of such universals will come from the systematic comparison of many different cultures, rather than from the absolute standards of classicism.

A second postulate of social anthropology is epistemological. It holds that the most reliable knowledge of people, societies, and cultures is to be had through directly acquainting oneself with them by personal observation, conversing with them in their own language, and living among them and sharing their mode of life for about a year at a time. This is usually called "field work" by social anthropologists, and is contrasted with "armchair speculation", hearsay evidence, "conjectural history" as well as with documentary history and archaeology, statistical surveys, and other indirect forms of evidence. In its strict sense, this postulate would restrict anthropological knowledge of a society to the period during which the anthropologist is actually observing it in the "field", and would exclude all reports of its previous states—bartering, as Firth says, space for time.

In epistemology, this doctrine has been called "radical empiricism" by William James, and leads logically to "a solipsism of the present moment." Its anthropological version may also have been influenced, as Murray Wax has suggested, by the "verstehen" and "empathy" theories of social understanding[5]. In any case, Malinowski, Radcliffe-Brown, and other social anthropologists have stressed the indispensability of field work for learning about the "imponderabilia" of everyday life, the contextual meaning of situations, and "the native's point of view."

If social anthropologists adhered strictly to the second postulate, social anthropology would consist of a collection of reports of personal observations and "true experience. "There is a third postulate, however, which keeps social anthropology from becoming a genre of travel literature of reports of a vision quest. This postulate prescribes that field observations and reports thereof should be ordered in accordance with a particular set of theoretical conceptions and problems. The theoretical conception that has been most favored in social anthropology is that all aspects of a society and of its culture, are parts of an interrelated and interdependent system, with each part contributing to the functioning and maintenance of the whole system. While assertions of monastic causalty are generally avoided,most social anthropologists tend to assume that "social structure" as a structure of social groups, or a network of social relations, is somehow more "basic" than other aspects of a socio-cultural system and that these other aspects can be "explained" by relating them to the social structure.

Stated in this form, the postulate of "structural-functional" analysis is not especially distinctive of social anthropology. As Kingsley Davis has recently observed, it is also found in sociology, economics, and political science, and in its generic form, in all scientific analysis of systems.[6]

What distinguishes structural-functional analysis in social anthropology from other disciplines is the disposition to apply it to small communities as wholes, and to assume that the primary building block of a society is the family group. Characteristically, a social-anthropological monograph seeks to demonstrate, through intensive field study of a small community, how religion, politics, economics, and all other "aspects" of society and culture are related to family, lineage, and clan organization. The postulate may therefore be called "micro-structural holism"; it assumes that the small community of a field study can be analyzed as a "primitive isolate."

The choice of a small community as a unit for the application of structural-functional analysis is not a logical consequence of structural-functional theory. Nor is it, as Radcliffe-Brown and others have held, simply a matter of practical convenience in the selection of a suitable unit for field work. The choice has been dictated by the assumption that "primary face-to-face groups" (especially the family) are the elementary bricks of all societies, and by the convergent influence of the first two postulates: that social anthropology is the study of "little" people by direct observation. The three postulates then appear to coincide in a definition of the object of study, the methods for studying it, and the theoretical conception about its structure and function. Social anthropology, in short, should study the everyday activities of ordinary people as an interdependent social system through intensive field work in small communities.

Is a "Social Anthropology of Civilizations" Possible?

The relevance of a discipline committed to the methodological postulates of populism, radical empiricism, and a microstructural holism, tor a comparative study of civilizations, is problematic. A "social anthropology of civilization" would appear to be a contradiction in terms, for civilizations are large-scale aggregates of social and cultural organizations in space and time, in which the activities and "high cultures" of different kinds of elites are as important as the "popular" culture of the ordinary people.

It is difficult to see, for example, how a civilization which met most of Gordon-Childe's criteria for early civilization—cities, writing, monumental art, full-time specialists, differentiated class system, etc.—could be studied without the use of evidence from archaeology, history, literature, linguistics and philology, and iconography, as well as demography, architecture, and the fine arts. And it is even more difficult to see how field work among small communities of villagers, who may have remained within the orbit of such a civilization, can uncover such evidence or, for that matter, the evidence of political, economic, and social organization characteristic of the civilization.

Some social anthropologists are quite prepared to accept the limitations imposed on their discipline by the methodological postulates. They would restrict social anthropology to a comparative study of "primitive" or "simple" societies and cultures and would leave the study of "complex" societies and cultures, and of civilizations, to other disciplines. Most social anthropologists, however, are not disposed to follow such a self-restraining ordinance. They do claim some relevance of social anthropology for the study of complex societies and civilizations, but they do not all agree on what kind of relevance.

One group sees the relevance as discovering universal "elementary" and "simple" principles for the the analysis of complex cases. Durkheim, for example, claimed that by a study of the "elementary forms" of religion in Australian totemism one could arrive at underlying principles that also hold for all religions. This claim continues to be echoed in later social anthropological studies of primitive religion.[7] It is really a form of the belief earlier stated by Radcliffe-Brown, that social anthropology seeks general social laws whose operation is most clearly seen in simple and primitive societies. Evans-Pritchard and some other social anthropologists have recently challenged both the intention and realization of such a claim for social anthropology, but most social anthropologists probably still tacitly accept it.

The expression of a hope in the *potential* relevance of social anthropology for civilizational studies while actually studying "primitive" and simple societies, has seemed to many, among social anthropologists and others alike, a highly utopian program. More direct studies of or within civilizations have therefore been undertaken. Some of these have tried to retain all of the methodological postulates intact, while others have modified one or more of the postulates:

The relevance of such studies for the wider societies and cultures depends on making a number of assumptions:

1. that the influences impinging on the small community from the wider society are so negligible that they can be disregarded or that they can be treated as extraneous "disturbances";

2. that what is found to be true of the small community can be projected onto the larger society and culture on the assumption that the small community is "representative" or a "microcosm" of the larger society; and

3. that a civilization consists of a collection of small communities, or that if it does not, the small community study at least provides insight into the building blocks of a civilization.

These assumptions are usually made by social anthropologists who have identified the small community selected for field study with the model of "the primitive isolate." They restrict social anthropological analysis of civilizations to microscopic community studies. That neither the community study nor social anthropology need be so restricted is becoming evident from the extensions of social anthropological studies to India, Japan, Latin America, and elsewhere. In these studies both the model of "the primitive isolate" and the special assumptions that go with it are being challenged. In fact, as social anthropologists move into "area" and civilizational studies the precise boundaries of their discipline become problematic.[8]

Decline of the "Primitive Isolate"

As social anthropologists have completed small community studies in India, Japan, and Southeast Asia, their confidence in these assumptions has been shaken: they have encountered increasing difficulty in applying the model of the "primitive isolate." Particular villages were found to be connected by many networks of social relations to other villages, to towns, and to urban centers. And as the variations among villages become better known, the selection of a "representative" or "typical" village was seen to be increasingly dependent on some predesignated set of attributes presumably characteristic of the whole society at a given time or throughout the entire history of the civilization. These attributes cannot be demonstrated by village studies. Historical and cultural studies, census surveys and other supra-village studies are required to determine these attributes.

Faced with such complications, some social anthropologists have struggled heroically to study complex societies and civilizations without abandoning their methodological postulates. A good representative of this group is F. G. Bailey, who has done important village studies in India in which he has related village social structure and culture to supra-village-level politics and economics.[9]

Yet, in a self-conscious analysis of his own work, Bailey is quite anxious to defend his disciplinary purity.[10] He is prepared to admit that in studying a village in India, in Latin America, or in Britain, the social anthropologist has moved into a field more complex than that of the "primitive isolate." He also admits that the events which he considers in a village "are also part of a literate tradition, and of a known sequence of historical events, and are appropriated and studied by economists and political scientists."[11]

In relation to the problem Bailey uses to illustrate his analysis, he cites two disputes between untouchables and clean castes in two villages he has studied. He notes that a knowledge of Hindu culture and values (especially concerning untouchability, vegetarianism, and the sacred cow); a knowledge of the villager's relations with the government administration, politicians, and merchants outside of the village; and a knowledge of the recent history of Gandhi's movement to abolish untouchability, and of India's political history since independence—all these are indispensable to an understanding of why the village disputes occurred at all and why they took a different course in the two villages.

Granting all this, Bailey is still not prepared to relax his conscience as a social anthropologist to assume responsibility for any of this necessary knowledge. The culture and values of Hinduism can be studied, Bailey recognizes, in the sacred and classical literature, in religious centers, and by specialists. But such study belongs to Indology and related disciplines, he says. He does not believe it is necessary for him as a social anthropologist to study this "great tradition" of Hinduism or its specific connections with the "little tradition" in the villages, in order to understand the role of the village temple and Hindu values in the disputes. He can, he believes, take Hindu culture and values as "givens" and go on to trace their effects in the village. The elementary knowledge of "the little tradition" as it appears at the village level, he can acquire "partly from reading about the manners and customs of the people of India, and partly (and more satisfactorily) by seeing how people behave and listening to the explanations they give of that behaviour."[12]

Aware that this attitude may appear philistine, Bailey tries to justify it as a necessity of specialization in problem, interest, and discipline.

"To explain culture traits in a village by relating them, either genetically or through morphological similarity to traits described in the sacred literature or found in the courts of kings or in the great religious centers, is another problem, different from the one with which I am concerned. It is a cultural problem which is left behind, unanswered and not needing to be answered, in the process of abstracting a system of social behaviour."[13]

Bailey deals with the villager's external political and economic relations and with the historical background in analogous fashion. These are also taken as "givens" for purposes of analyzing village social relations. The analysis of the "givens" he relegates to other disciplines, to political science, economics, and history. Even if the social anthropologist should be naive and mistaken about the nature of these "givens," "a wrong diagnosis of anterior causes will not—in the case of "given" events invalidate (his) analysis of their effects in the social system of the villages."[14]

In spite of his plea that social anthropologists who study villages in civilized countries should follow a policy of learned ignorance, Bailey is not so naive as to believe that it can be followed strictly.

"It is clear that, even if in our analyses of social regularities the cultural facts and the historical background are left tacitly unconsidered, it would be foolish not to know as many of these facts as we can."[15]

Short of becoming an Indologist or a historian, he is willing to consider each case on its own.

"A sociological study of a Buddhist monastery is likely to require considerable familiarity with sacred literature, while field work among a tribe such as the Chenchus would require practically none."[16]

This almost sounds as if Bailey is willing for social anthropology to move out of the village to study problems that may require some changes in its techniques and concepts. And he does refer to social anthropological studies of problems in a factory, or a mining township, or a parliamentary assembly as requiring changes in techniques. But he makes it quite plain that as the social anthropologist undertakes research into supra-village relations and groups—a feasible and logical next step in research for him—he will need to restrict his research to those groups which are held together by "multiplex" links of kinship, ritual, politics and the like, if he is to remain a social anthropologist.[17] Bailey believes that as extra-village relations increase and become important, the social anthropologist must be prepared to analyze these relations by his own techniques or "by techniques and concepts which he may devise to analyze them; otherwise he runs the risk of losing touch with contemporary reality."[18]

There are other social anthropologists who, starting with a field study of an Indian village, have been less reticent than Bailey about combining other disciplines with their studies. Louis Dumont uses Indology, Bernard Cohn history, McKim Marriot sociological Indology, Scarlett Epstein economics, and so on. The differences between these social anthropologists and Bailey is not simply a difference in training, personal interest, or the problems they happen to have chosen to work on, although such differences do exist. Nor is it merely a matter of attitude towards interdisciplinary research. The real issues concern the conception of social anthropology and how far it needs to be modified for a study of civilizations.

Bailey begins by accepting all three methodological postulates—social anthropology is essentially a field study of the micro-system of social relations in village communities. Recognizing that the system of social relations in an Indian village cannot be satisfactorily explained without reference to supra-village "givens," he is prepared to move into the study of micro-systems of social relations outside of the village. He does not see such an expansion of social anthropology, however, as requiring any modification in the other two postulates; he seems to assume that essentially the same techniques of field work among ordinary people will suffice. By the same token, he sees no necessity for the inclusion of history, Indology, political science, economics, or any other disciplines as essential components in the training of a social anthropologist, although these other disciplines must be invoked to account for the "givens" which the social anthropologist cannot analyze.

One complication of Bailey's position is that the social anthropologist needs to take some account of culture, history, politics, and economics even when he is studying village social structure. Whether he undertakes to train himself in the relevant disciplines or collaborates with other specialists in these disciplines is of less significance, to my mind, than the recognition that the village is not a "primitive isolate" from which social structure can be abstracted as a self-contained unit or theoretical analysis. If this is so for study of problems at the village level, how much more so is an interdisciplinary approach called for in the study of supra-village problems, or in the study of an entire civilization. A social anthropologist may, of course, renounce any interest in these problems as being beyond his disciplinary jurisdiction, or he may, as Bailey does, try to select such problems as will require a minimal modification of his postulates, or he may be prepared to change the postulates as far as is necessary to study civilizations comparatively. Robert Redfield's work, to which we now turn, illustrates a movement toward this last position.

Civilizations as Societal and Cultural Structures

In Indian studies the recognition that the peasant village did not fit the social anthropologist's theoretical model of the "primitive isolate" and did not contribute a suitable field unit for the application of "micro-structural holistic" analysis came about in 1954 when a group of leading social anthropologists considered the question in relation to their own field work in Indian villages.[19] Social anthropologists working in other countries came to a similar conclusion about the same time.[20]

This recognition marked a turning point in the development of social anthropology. For some it meant the end of the classical tight-little-island kind of social anthropology and perhaps the end of further creative development for any kind of social anthropology. Others saw in the situation new problems and new opportunities for the adaptation of the techniques and concepts of social anthropology. If the peasant village was not a good unit for micro-structural-functional analysis it was still a good unit of field work and a manageable point of entry for the study of a civilization. The abandonment of the small community as the unit of theoretical analysis liberated it as a unit of field study for a great variety of non-village groups. Field studies could thus be undertaken in "small communities" of political leaders, industrialists, priests, and urban classes, without assuming that these were closed structural systems or "primitive isolates." Many other kinds of studies—cultural, historical, archaeological— also became legitimate and relevant for a social anthropological study of a civilization. New theoretical frameworks were developed to guide these new kinds of studies.

One of the first social anthropologists to recognize the limitation of the "primitive isolate" model was Robert Redfield. Ironically, Redfield is widely considered as an advocate of this model through his writings on the "folk society" and "the little community." His contribution, on the contrary, consists in extending social anthropology beyond this model to a study of civilizations. Since Redfield's ideas and field studies were developed over a thirty to forty-year period, his position has been frequently misunderstood.

His first field study in 1926 in Tepoztlán, Mexico, was designed as a study of a peasant community, a type of society intermediate between the tribal societies usually studied by anthropologists and the cities usually studied by sociologists. Since a majority of mankind lived in such "intermediate societies," it would be useful, he believed, to study them as organized, functioning wholes. Although he refers in this first work to some folk-like characteristics of the community, he did not yet have at this time the concept of the "folk society" or of the "folk culture" as ideal types in contrast to a concept of "urban" type of society and culture. Oscar Lewis' criticism of the Tepoztlán study from this point of view is therefore anachronistic.

The "folk urban" typology enters the picture only in the early 1930's as a theoretical framework to guide the comparative studies of four communities in Yucatan. As Redfield himself has repeatedly emphasized, this typology was not intended to glorify the "folk society" or even to classify particular societies as "folk" or "urban." It was developed rather as an abstract theoretical conception of the nature and process of social and cultural differentiation underlying the growth of civilization, in terms of a set of ideas derived from Sir Henry Maine, Fustel de Coulanges, Tönnies, Durkheim, and Max Weber, among others.

In the Yucatan studies, Redfield and his associates used this theoretical framework to ask questions about the degree to which "folk" or "urban" traits of society and culture occur in a tribal village, a peasant village, a small town, and a capital city—all compared and studied simultaneously. They were also interested in the order of variation in traits as one passes from tribal village to city and in whether the variations in some traits were regularly dependent on variations in other traits. The findings of the Yucatan study were that the sequence and frequency of incidence of traits did follow the geographical sequence of communities on the map, and that the generalization could be postulated as a hypothesis that as isolation and cultural homogeneity decrease, individualism and cultural disorganization would increase.

These findings were not taken to establish the existence of a "folk-urban" *dichotomy* but rather of a "folk-urban" *continuum*, since the city had some folk-like traits and the villages some urban-like traits. The question in each case was the degree of incidence, predominance, and constellation of traits in relation to the sequence of communities compared. The significant contribution of the Yucatan study was that it introduced a theoretical framework which transcended the "primitive isolate" and applied this framework in field research to a particular sequence of communities. To use the language later introduced by urban geographers, Redfield was trying to deal in the Yucatan studies with an "urban hierarchy of central places," or "a system of cities."

There were, however, two constraints imposed on the concept of a civilization" in the Yucatan studies that were to be removed in later work. "Civilization" was identified chiefly with the flow of modern, Western urban influences into the city of Merida and from Merida into its hinterland. Redfield denies explicitly that he was doing a diffusion study, but he does not deny that he was studying the interaction (or "acculturation") of modern, urban, Western civilization with the "folk culture" of Yucatan.

Although historical materials are used in the study and suggestions for historical extrapolations are offered, Redfield also denies that he was doing history in the Yucatan study. He insists, rather, on the methodological constraint of synchronic comparison : placing the different communities side by side as if they existed only at the time of observation. This is a form of "radical empiricism," but it is applied in this case not to a single little community but to several communities of increasing scale and requiring the combined observations of a number of people. It is also interesting that in the Yucatan studies the methodological postulates of "populism" and "structural-functional holism" are extended to a wider field than the "primitive isolate" but are not abrogated. Redfield does not use the concepts of "social structure" and "function" in the study in precisely Radcliffe-Brown's or Malinowski's sense. But he has already made an explicit and consistent distinction between "culture" as a set of conventionalized understandings and "society", and he thought of communities as organized, functioning systems.[21]

The methodological constraints of the Yucatan study were first dropped in *The Primitive World and Its Transformations*. In this work the concepts of "folk society" and "folk culture" are retained as ideas practically unchanged from their earlier forms. But they are no longer contrasted simply with modern urban, Western civilization. Instead, another concept of "indigenous civilization" is introduced into the theoretical scheme. An indigenous civilization is formed out of local folk cultures and societies with some syncretism of foreign elements but without loss of its moral and cultural integration. It is characterized by a public and state-managed "moral order," speculative intellectual developments by professional *literati* and state cults in both town and city. In indigenous civilizations the "moral order" can prevail over the "technical order," Redfield believes. because of the slow rate of development of technical order and relative isolation of the civilization from external contacts. Early Mesopotamia and Egypt and the Maya before the Spanish conquest are approximations of "indigenous civilizations."

And "indigenous civilization" includes the *peasant* type of society and culture as a transformation of those folk societies and cultures that have come under the influence of towns and cities. The "peasant" is a cultivator of land who has, over many hundreds of years, developed a way of life around the land. The "peasant" type of village is part-folk and part-urban. It maintains permanent economic, political, social, and cultural relations with neighboring town and cities, but it is also "inward looking" as is the folk village. Measured by the ideal "peasant" type, Redfield now sees Tepoztlán and Chan Kom more "peasant" than "folk-like" villages. This is not inconsistent with his previous characterization of these villages as folk-like, since he did not then construct a peasant type to mark an intermediate point on the folk-urban continuum. It is true to say both that Chan Kom is more peasant than folk and that it is more folk than urban.

Modern, urban, Western civilization which in the Yucatan studies was the ideal type contrasted with the "folk society" is also represented in the later theoretical scheme as a species of secondary civilization." This type of civilization results from a rapid development of the technical order or from increasing contacts and communications, or from both conditions. It is characterized by unrest and loss of moral certainty, by rationalism and scepticism, and by the rise of new ethical and religious systems. Rome from the Second Punic War to the end of the Republic, and Merida, in the 1930's, are both given as examples of cities undergoing "secondary civilization."

Under conditions of relative isolation and slow technical development, and indigenous civilization that has once experienced "secondary civilization" may again reintegrate its folk, peasant, and urban communities and cultures. Redfield believes that this is what happened to Maya villages and towns after the Spanish conquest "decapitated" the indigenous Maya civilization. Indigenous Mayan elements fused with Spanish elements to produce a "remade" folk and peasant culture. This did not occur in Merida, however, where the influences of "secondary civilization" prevailed. In this perspective, the Yucatan studies appear as studies of the effects of the West as a "secondary civilization" on a remade moral order in which the indigenous civilization's top layer is missing.

Some further implications of this revised theoretical framework are traced in "The Cultural Role of Cities," *Peasant Society and Culture* and in several later papers. Since these have been discussed elsewhere,[22] the present discussion will emphasize the implications for a social anthropological concept of "civilization." The "folk-urban" continuum has become in the revised scheme a "folk-civilization" continuum. The continuum, moreover, is not linear and singular but plural and connected. Groups of folk societies and their local cultures under favorable conditions of relative isolation, mutual contacts, slow technical development, and occasional external stimulus give rise to towns and cities in which different classes of specialists manage the more complex forms of social and political organization and develop a more systematic and speculative "great tradition" from the "little tradition" of the local folk cultures. As some of these folk societies became permanently dependent on the towns and cities, the "peasant" appears as a new social and cultural type.

This "primary" phase of urbanization and civilization gives way to a "secondary" phase as increasing contacts and communications bring in new religions, idea systems, technologies, and forms of political organization. Depending on the rate and character of change, these new influences set in motion forces which tend to disintegrate the "primary civilization," its "great tradition" and social order. Under favorable conditions, these forces may be counteracted by others making for continuity and new forms of reintegrated folk, peasant, and urban societies and cultures.

With the theoretical scheme no longer restricted to a synchronic perspective, the "folk-civilization" continua can now be interpreted as recurrent historical processes through which particular civilizations get formed from local folk societies and cultures at many different places and times.

We can now state in more abstract language the conception of "a civilization" that is implied by this theoretical scheme. "A civilization" is not identified with any particular kind of community, form of social relations, social class, or kind of cultural product or capacity such as writing. It is, rather, the total structure of communities—folk, peasant, and urban—and the networks of social relations which bind these communities together within a particular civilization, its "societal structure." The boundaries of such a structure of networks and centers cannot be precisely delimited in space and time although they extend through space and time. Political, linguistic, religious, and ideological boundaries are equally imprecise for delimiting the structure and complex historical growth of a civilization. Kroeber has suggested that the best delimitation of a civilization is given by its dominant style or total pattern of all its constituent culture patterns. This suggestion has been taken up by Toynbee in his later work.[23]

The stylistic characterization of civilization does not pre-suppose any "societal structure," although Toynbee does pre-suppose it; it is in any case pretty far removed from the concepts and methods of social anthropology.

Within the Redfield model, the problem of the delimination, identify, and continuity of a civilization is handled in terms of the notion of "cultural structure." The cultural structure of a particular civilization consists of the structure of its cultural traditions and the structure of its thought and values. This structure, for any civilization, is always compounded of "great" and "little" dimensions in mutual interaction and influence. It is organized and transmitted through specific media and agents, in particular centers and networks, i.e., through a specific "organization of tradition." The "cultural structure" of civilization is thus the compliment of its "societal structure." The entire societal structure of social networks and centers is given a distinctive identity by the "cultural content," the systems of thought and value, which circulate through it. And these systems of thought and values are given a local habitation and a name by the "cultural structure," i.e., the organized channels, institutions, and agents involved in the transmission of the "cultural content." The extent of a particular civilization in space and time is measured, therefore, not by the spread of isolated cultural traits but by each of its "cultural structure" as a transmitter of its characteristic systems of thought and value.

Redfield's social anthropological approach to the comparative study of civilizations has, guided research on the rise of early civilizalions,[24] on the unity and variety of Muslim civilization,[25] on the role of Confucianism in Chinese civilization,[26] on the relation of Hinduism to tribal, peasant, and urban culture in India,[27] on the social applications and roles of Hinduism, Islam, and animism in Javanese religion,[28] and many other recent comparative studies in different civilizations.[29] Since that approach is exploratory and highly tentative we can expect further extensions and modifications of it.

Rather than try to prophesy the future shape of these, let us return in conclusion to the question of Redfield's reluctance to insist that his approach was "a social anthropology of civilizations." The preceding discussion indicates that there are some grounds for this reluctance, for his concepts and methods certainly go beyond the "primitive isolate" of classical social anthropology. On the other hand, his extensions of social anthropological concepts and methods to the study of civilization are at every point logical and natural. "Societal structure" is a natural extension of Radcliffe-Brown's concept of "social structure" and "cultural structure" makes some use of Firth's concept of social organization." He did not reject the three methodological postulates, but extended their applications to a wider range of people, communities, and kinds of evidence. Field studies of little communities are not precluded from "folk-civilization" studies but are rather integrated with historical, cultural, and other kinds of studies relevant for tracing the "societal structures" and "cultural structures" of particular civilizations. The positive aspects of classical social anthropology have been incorporated into a wider social anthropology of civilizations, and only the negative restrictions have been dropped.

The issue is more than the semantic one of the proper way to define "social anthropology." Social anthropology is itself a cultural tradition that grows and changes. Which changes introduce radical discontinuities with the "essential" principles of the tradition and which are continuous with those principles is a matter of judgment for the "carriers" of the tradition. Social anthropologists who make these judgments primarily in terms of the conformity of their discipline to the three methodogical postulates, however run the risk of making that discipline as isolated from contemporary, past, and future realities as the model of the "primitive isolate" has become. Social anthropologists, on the other hand, who are prepared to extend and modify their concepts and methods for a study of peasant and urban communities and historic civilizations are creating a new kind of social anthropology which studies "great traditions" and "great societies," as well as "little traditions" and "little communities", and which is willing to use in these studies the evidence of history, archaeology, literature, and the arts, as well as the evidence of direct personal observation.

The "new" social anthropology will be concerned with both the everyday activities of the common people and the sophisticated creations of the elite as an interdependent social structure and cultural organization, and will be dependent on both intensive studies of small communities and urban aggregates, in macro-holistic terms. If the resulting picture is not so neatly circumscribed and unified as are our studies of the "primitive isolate", it will be closer to the complex reality that is in fact modern civilization.

Notes

1. *Peasant Society and Culture* esp. chap. 1 ; three lectures on civilization reprinted in *Human Nature and Society* ; *The Little Community* and *The Primitive World and Its Transformation*. The collaboration with philosophers of history, historians of particular civilizations, linguists, philosophers, and other anthropologists was organized in a special project supported by the Ford Foundation from 1951 to 1961. Some of the results of this collaboration have been published in the series, *Comparative Studies In Cultures and Civilization*, University of Chicago Press. See Milton Singer, "The Social Organization of Indian Civilization," Diogones, 1964, for further references. I am indebted to Fred Eggan, Benard Cohn, Margaret Redfield and Murray Wax for helpful comments.

2. *Cf.* Isiah Berlin on Herder in *Encounter*, 1965.

3. Franz Boas, *Race, Language and Culture*, 1940 (reprinted 1966), pp. 306-312. See also G.W. Stocking Jr., in *Journal of the History of the Behavioral Sciences* 1, (1965) for Boas', reaction to German "high culture".

4. See, e.g. William Ridgeway, "The Relation of Anthropology to the Classical Studies", (Presidential Address to the Royal Anthropological Institute), *Journal of the Royal Anthropological* Institute, (1909)

5. Murray Wax, "Religion and Magic", mimeo., 1965.

6. Kingsley Davis, "The Myth of Functional Analysis as a Special Method in Sociology and Social Anthropology," *American Sociological Review*, 24 (1959).

7. M. Gluckman, ed., *Closed Systems and Open Minds*, 1964.

8. See Milton Singer, "The Social Sciences in non-Western Studies," *Annals*, 356 (1964), pp. 30, 44.

9. F.G. Bailey, *Caste and and the Economic Frontier*, 1957 ; *Tribe Caste and Nation*, 1960 ; *Politics and Social Change*, Orissa 1959, 1963 ; "Two Villages in Orissa" in Gluckman, *op. cit.* 1964.

10. F.G. Bailey in Gluckman, *op. cit.*

11. *Ibid.*, p. 80.

12. *Ibid.*, p. 61.

13. *Ibid.*, p. 64.

14. *Ibid.*, p. 70.

15. *Ibid.*, p. 81.

16. *Ibid.*,

17. *Ibid.*, pp. 78, 79.

18. *Ibid.*, p. 79.

19. See McKim Marriott, ed., *Village India*, 1955.

20. See J. Barnes, "Class and Committees in a Norwegian Island Parish" *Human Relations* 7 (1954). E. Leach, *The Political Systems of Highland Burma*, 1954, Robert Redfield, *The Little Community*, 1955 ; *Peasant Society and Culture*, 1956 ; Clifford Geertz., "Studies in Peasant Life ; Community and Society" in B.J. Siegel ed., *Biennial* Review of Anthropology, 1961; M. Friedman, "A Chinese Phase in Social Anthropology," *British Journal of Sociology*, 14 (1963).

21. See. e.g., Robert Redfield, *The Folk Culture of Yucatan,* 1941 pp. 15-16.

22. Milton Singer, *Diogenes*, 1964, *op. cit.*

23. A.L. Kroeber, *Style and Civilizations*, 1957 ; *An Anthropologist Looks at History*, 1963 ; Arnold Toynbee, *Reconsiderations*, 1963, pp. 287-91.

24. R. Braidwood and G.R. Willey, *Courses Toward Urban Life*, 1962 ; Braidwood, "Levels in Prehistory" ed., in Sol Tax, ed., *Evolution after Darwin*, II 1960 ; Braidwood, "Prelude to Civilization," in C.H. Kraeling *City Invincible,* 1960.

25. Gustav von Grunebaum, ed., *Unity and Variety in Muslim Civilization,* 1955.

26. Arthur Wright, ed., *Confucianism and Chinese Civilization,* 1964.

27. S. Sinha, "Tribe-Caste and Tribe-Peasant Continua in Central India," *Man in India*, 45 (1965) ; Milton Singer, ed., *Traditional India ; Structure and Change,* 1958, 1959.

28. Clifford Geertz, *The Religion of Java*, 1960.

29. M. Orans, *The Santal, A Tribe in Search of a Great Tradition,* 1965 ; Bernard Cohn and McKim Marriott, "Networks and Centres in the Integration of Indian Civilization," Journal of Social Research 1 (1958) ; Milton Singer, ed., *Krishna ; Myths, Rites and Attitudes,* 1966 ; M.N. Srinivas, *Social Change in Modern India*, 1965.

Comparative Literature Studies, Critical and Historical—Some Possibilities and Some Limits

GEORGE L. ANDERSON*

"The term 'comparative' literature is troublesome," say Wellek and Warren in *Theory of Literature*,[1] and that is "doubtless, indeed, why this important mode of literary study has had less than the expected academic success." The author—this is Wellek's chapter—then goes on to discuss the various kinds of research activity that have been called "comparative." One of these is the study of oral literature, which for some time now has not limited its concerns to the migration and transmutation of motifs and themes but has also produced sophisticated analyses both of forms and of the narrator-audience interaction, borrowing techniques from the structural approaches of the now old "new critics" and also from anthropology.

Another more common meaning of the term "comparative literature," Wellek observes, confines itself to the relationships between two or more literatures. The father of this was perhaps Fernand Baldensperger and the mother the *Revue de littérature acomparée*. The accomplishments of this school for more than a quarter of a century are too well known to need elaboration here, and the increasing sterility of the approach in its more mechanical applications brought about a decline of scholarly interest in comparative studies, from which we have been partially rescued by journals and conferences devoted as much to literary theory in its international setting as to literary influence across national boundaries. Wellek rightly notes that there is no methodological justification for regarding a study of Poe's influence on Baudelaire as "comparative" and one on Dryden's influence on Pope as—what ? "Non-comparative" ?

Finally, the concept of "comparative literature" as the study of literature in its totality—"world literature," "general literature", "universal literature"—is scrutinized. Wellek distinguishes between the visionary "one world" literature of the future envisioned by Goethe and the notion that we should study the literature of each individual nation or language enclave, the latter view held by the founders of *Books Abroad*.

---

*George L. Anderson was Associate Executive Secretary of the Modern Language Association of America. He is Editor of *Masterpieces of the Orient* and author of various articles. He was Co-Director of the Indiana Conference on Oriental-Western Literary Relations in 1954, and is now Chairman of the English Department of the University of Hawaii.

We can add much evidence to Wellek's that "world literature"—whatever that may mean—is certainly the modern, popular extension of "comparative literature" and comes first to the minds of the college teacher and study of today. Some of this development has come since *Theory of Literature* was first published in 1942, but the idea that we should not neglect any of the world's literatures has its monuments in the multi-volumed histories of the literatures of the world produced from the turn of the century to the *Handbuch der Literaturwissenschaft* of Walzel in the 1920's. Some great works have survived in usefulness from these series : Browne's Persian, Nicholson's Arabic, Winternitz's Indian, Florenz's Japanese volumes. (It is worth noting that the Asian scholars writing for these early series seem to have written for the ages and the scholars on Western literature for a day.)

We now have college departments of world literature and one can even feel guilty about being caught neglecting the literature of any country or region. At a recent comparative literature meeting, the agonized cry went up : "What about the literature of Africa ? Why are we neglecting it ?" One is tempted here to make an analogy with the problems the food editor of the *New York Times* faces because of his democratic notion that every country of the world has at least one or two foods worth eating. The editor is forced to print, annually, recipes for dundee haggis and oat-meal when duty calls him to Scotland. Any gourmet faced with these would regard Samuel Johnson as a Scottish patriot. Literature is doubtless a different kind of food, and the study of the literature of any country is worthwhile and may illuminate literature in general. For the kind of comparative studies proposed here, however, the usefulness of both the minor literatures and the literatures not yet systematically studied is limited.

Before leaving Wellek, it is interesting to note that when he wishes to select works of general literary historiography—literary history "on a supernational scale"—he cites Ernst Robert Curtius' *European Literature and the Latin Middle Ages*[2] and Erich Auerbach's *Mimesis*.[3] The choice is not surprising. Both are works of marvelous erudition and critical sense ; both were done by scholars with superb linguistic gifts. Curtius' study, however, is confined to the European scene at a particularly unified period of cultural history. And Auerbach traces a single concept—that of reality—though he ranges from Homer to James Joyce within the European tradition. These two works, even if there were not others, demonstrate the value of and the new spirit in comparative studies. Curtius' chronological span is narrower, and he can attempt comprehensiveness. Auerbach's chronological span is the entire history of the West, and he limits himself to a concept.

If these examples are acceptable, our question ought to be : Does the success of the comparative method depend on confining the work to one cultural tradition, here either one as large as the entire Western tradition or smaller like the Western medieval tradition? Can significant studies in general literary historiography result from comparing Sanskrit literature with Greek, Chinese and Japanese with European ? We are not here referring to the two other kinds of comparative studies defined above, the tracing of motifs and themes—"The Ulysses Theme in Japan," for example, as the subject of one article—or the influence of literature or writer x on writer or literature y—Meredith on Soseki, Whitman on modern Chinese poetry. Is it useful on any level from the stylistic to the broadest philosophical and historical to attempt, comparative investigations of literatures not culturally related and how might one go about doing it ?

It is necessary to think of the literary object as something partly bound within a specific language. That is to say, some of the literary effects are possible to comprehend only in the original language and are essentially untranslatable, though sometimes they may be cleverly imitated. Some literary effects possible in other languages, moreover, are denied the poet, or if he attempts them, he may fare badly. Finally, what the poet *thinks* are the strengths and weaknesses of his native tongue can have considerable bearing on his practice.

At issue here are literary phenomena which can be described in linguistic terms. Rhyme, for instance, has been considered by some English poets and critics as especially good in the English language and by German poets and critics as especially good in German. The French, as we know, regard it with suspicion; the greatest Latin poetry does not have it. It is used in Chinese, but because of the number of homophones, the poet must be subtle and in some forms correlate his rhyme with patterns of tones elsewhere in the poem.

Alliteration is a conspicuous metrical device in some poets and even in some periods of English literary history. Alliteration is easy to identify, but we have not much studied the kind of half-alliteration we get in English by alternating *t* and *d*, *ch*, and *k*, *p*, and *b*, though Jakobson and other linguists have given us the mechanism for identifying these phonemic near-relationships.

There is no precise term for what we are discussing here. Style is perhaps the best term, but stylistic features that can be recognized as phonemic, morphemic or tangememic but not semantic. In this area of style we need literary studies which would attempt to determine the actual devices of poetic style in a given language or more narrowly in the corpus of a single poet or school, with prose samplings as a control. What devices are used ? How frequently ? How are they used in conjuction with one another ? Probably only a computerized analysis would give us this.

We should compare this with the results of a systematic survey of what the poets and critics *think* are the characteristics of poetic style as against non-poetic style. A more complex form of these studies would be to determine the actual style of a poet influenced by a foreign style or by the conscious revival of the earlier modes of his own language, and compare this with his theory of it. Such studies would be preliminary to a comparative study. We will not know whether or not it is useful to compare Chinese poetic style with Greek or French until there is a body of data sufficiently scientific to provide a basis for comparison.

There is probably no such thing as comparative poetics on the phonemic-morphemic-syntactic level and one is naturally reluctant to propose that a group of scholars devote much time and energy to proving the absolute non-existence of a now non-existent discipline. The preliminary stages of the investigation, however, would bring together systematically a mass of data on literary style in accordance with criteria established comparatively. Such a project would have to be a group effort, and the bulk to be done by advanced specialists would be at the beginning—drawing the blueprint, and at the end—evaluating the results.

Similar studies are desirable in the domain of semantics, especially in the identification of common figures of speech. The structure of the figure, its frequency, and what it is presumed to do aesthetically, are all of interest and can only be comparatively studied if criteria can be co-operatively developed. It is not being suggested that there is no scholar-critic in the country not capable of working equally well in English and, say, Japanese poetics, but only that cooperatively developed guidelines for extensive projects provide safeguards in terminology and methodology.

We have gotten beyond the elements of the literary work which are determined by and restricted by the language to what may be vaguely called the "translatable" components—logical structure, motifs, plots, semantic repetitions and so forth. Before going forward, it is necessary to deal with cliches, one of them of contemporary criticism, the other of the minds of the East and the West.

A dominating principle of modern literary criticism has been that the literary work is essentially verbal texture. This principle has its greatest validity in dealing with lyric poetry, and particularly with lyric poetry that is symbolic or ironic or ambiguous and rich in metaphor. It is no accident that modern poetry and the metaphysical poetry of the seventeenth century appealed most to the modern critics who founded the new criticism. Focusing on close analysis, these crltics would find it of little consequence that three versions of the Oedipus Rex legend would have at their core the same plot. But it is in terms of plot of course, that Aristotle defines the poet's function. He is a maker of narratives, not a musician and not the possessor of a magic word-hoard.

With their bias, the founding fathers of the new criticism tended to neglect fiction and especially drama, and the most provocative recent survey of the history of criticism—W.K. Wimsatt and Cleanth Brook's *Literary Criticism, A Short History*[4]—somewhat neglects fiction and drama. The relative importance of verbal texture versus plot and other structural components in a literary work cannot be determined, of course ; it can only be surmised. It is a matter for the literary theorist's intuition. It is safe to say that the relative importance varies with the work, but this is only saying what has often been said, that each literary object has to some extent its own set of norms. However, Aristotle's position is defensible, even if he thought, as he may have, that the summary of a story like the Oedipus Rex would be poetry and capable of producing catharsis.

We would not be happy today to see plot alone considered as the predominent structural element but would include all kinds of architectonic matters in the work above the level of verbal texture. In recent years some excellent analysis have appeared, such as Francis Fergusson's *The Idea of a Theater*,[5] Wayne Booth's *The Rhetoric of Fiction*,[6] and Northrop Frye's *Anatomy of Criticism*.[7] It would be interesting to see what use might be made of the methods used in these volumes by young scholars interested in Asian literatures. In any event, there is apparently much that can be said about the drama and the novel above the level of verbal texture, and above this level Asian and Western works are comparable. Though a comparison might not yield anything of interest, we will not know it until we try it.

Related to this increased interest in and more adequate machinery for the study of larger structural elements is a second observation. Any characterizing of the mental habits of the Asian and the Westerner is a hazardous affair, but I shall confine my remarks to literary critics and not apply them to human beings in general on the assumption that this sociological sub-class has not been widely investigated. The Western scholar of Asian literature seems to fear (wisely, he would say) comparisons between Asian and Western literary modes, movements, theories of art, and similar matters. He is conscious of the fact that the two traditions are unrelated historically and fears vagueness and the loose analogy. A question like, "Is there such a thing as classicism in Chinese literature?" is likely to bring the response: well, yes there is, but it differs so much from that which is called "classicism" in the West that a comparison is dangerous. This caution is commendable and should not necessarily be deprecated.

Conversely, many Asians writing literary criticism (the basis of my observation is Indian and Japanese critics writing in English) tend on the one hand to make comparisons which seem to us to be vaguely philosophical between Western and Asian works and on the other hand to argue, if pushed, that delicate matters of style are ineffable and cannot be explained to a Westerner. It may well be, however, that valuable elements in literature, even philosphical concepts, are broad enough to discuss comparatively. Perhaps less caution by Western scholars and more rigor on the part of Asian critics is needed.

The example just given, "classicism," is deliberately chosen to be a poor one. It is a broad term that needs to be defined anew by everyone who uses it. It includes aesthetic, sociological, and philosphical components. Some of the components however, would be worth investigating comparatively, using both Western and Asian literary materials. The revival of interest in antiquity is a historically demonstrable fact that does not have to be deduced from literary style. The imitation of literary styles of a particular period in the past if it is of the magnitude of a school or movement, is likewise identifiable. What are the literary theories offered for a drive towards a plain style in any literature? Is there an alleged scientific or philosophical basis for this? What are the social and political conditions surrounding such a movement? What do the leaders of the movement find objectionable in the styles they are attempting to displace?

There is the ebb and flow of subjectivity in writing, and the quantity of autobiographical content. What is the attitude of the culture during various periods to originality, "plagiarism," and translation? At various times in history both Western and Asian writers have redacted the matter of the past and have considered translation or paraphrase a laudable literary activity; at other times, this has been unfashionable. From these kinds of data we can start from a known point, and not carry into our investigation the burdens of omnibus Western critical terms like classicism, romanticism, baroque, and impressionism.

Let us now move on to a specific example of an Eastern literary concept shedding light on Western practice. This concerns the idea of what is called the "affective fallacy" and the Indian theory of *rasa*. The "affective fallacy" was promulgated most persuasively in an essay by W.K. Wimsatt, Jr. and Monroe C. Beardsley, published in the *Sewanee Review* in 1946. Wimsatt and Beardsley argue essentially that the effect of the literary work upon the reader is in the domain of audience psychology and cannot properly be analyzed by literary criticism. "The affective fallacy," they say, "is a confusion between the poem and its *results* (what it *is* and what it *does*), a special case of epistemological skepticism. It begins by trying to derive the standard of criticism from the psychological effects of the poem and ends in impressionism and relativism."[8]

This doctrine, though not universally accepted, has been a powerful weapon, especially pedagogically, against the, "How does the poem make me feel?" kind of impressionism that afflicted the nineteenth-century critics and that continues to harass the unwary teacher of literature. It is certainly true that the measurement of audience reaction is difficult or impossible. But if we assume that the dramatist proscribes a precise reaction in his every scene, then the individual variations on this required reaction are minimized. Sanskrit dramatic theory—the theory of *rasa*—is an affective theory, but I am not in a hurry to call it a fallacy.

What Wimsatt and Beardsley postulate seems to be true for Western drama. We are not sure how *katharsis* occurs in an audience. Presumably it is something which has happened by the time the play is over. Aristotle does not illuminate this matter. We cannot point to a passage and say, "Here is where *katharsis* occurs." In applying the Longinian concept of the sublime to drama, we can and indeed must point to a specific passage. Any emotional transport must emanate from a certain scene and a particular group of lines, but all of us cannot agree on the same lines—our judgment of this is subjective.

We cannot, however, be so subjective about Sanskrit or even Japanese drama. At least in certain scenes in the Noh play, the response is built into the play by the text, by symbolic gestures, and by long tradition. In Seami's play *Aoi No Ue*, the beautiful woman possessed by the demon of jealousy changes, before our eyes, into a hideous, two-horned demon. This is done on the stage by the actor changing masks, having hidden his face in the sleeves of his gown. It is impossible for the Noh actor to ring changes on this scene as they have been rung by Hamlet's first vision of his father's ghost by Betterton, Garrick, Mansfield, Irving, Evans, Gielgud, and Olivier. The hideousness of jealousy is in the play complex—in the text, in the accompanying acting and dancing, and especially in the sculptured and colored mask, and it is not determined by the audience or measured by the intensity of audience response. If there is no response it is either a bad performance or a bad audience. The dramatist expects in large part a stock response and programs the play to achieve this.

This is not to say that the member of the audience is not entitled to his own variations on the assigned emotion or that he is not entitled to the connoisseur's subjective appreciation of emotional refinements, the nature of which is less easy to agree upon. It is only to say that the dramatist tells us what emotions—at least what major emotions—to anticipate, expects us to receive them, and is supported in this by tradition.

The ultimate in systematic affective theory is the Indian theory of *rasa*. This concept goes back to the fourth century *Natyashastra* of the semi-legendary Bharata—the Thespis, as it were, of Sanskrit drama—but is most clearly enunciated in the *Dasharupa* of Dhanamjaya of the tenth century. The play is conceived of as dominated by a single emotional flavor (*rasa* is sometimes translated "sentiment" but "flavor" is better). The number of dominant emotional flavors is usually reckoned as eight, but the highest types of drama employ either the heroic or the erotic. A most elaborate system of classification has been developed to demonstrate the nature of all human emotions and the means by which these can be transmitted from the author through the actors to the audience.

If the Aristotlian drama is conceived as a plot line of rising and falling action representable by a bar graph, the Sanskrit drama is a colored wash of dominant emotion overlaid with differently colored subordinate emotions. Thus the *rasa* of Kalidasa's *Shakuntala* is that of love, but jealousy, surprise, wonder, and grief arise at various stages of the plot. One should be able to point to a scene and identify its emotions as they occur sequentially (all possible or at least all dramatically legitimate emotions are listed in the *Dasharupa*).

This is not a dramatic theory of the imitation of an action but of an imitation of a state of being. There is in the play, an "objective correlative"—to use Eliot's term—which produces a generalized emotion in the spectator if the play is well performed and if the audience is up to the level of appreciation required. The audience, furthermore, is cued to emotions by an elaborate vocabulary of formalized gestures. At the beginning of the *Shakuntala* we know that the King has received a good omen because we are told that his right arm throbs. Since the play is in the erotic *rasa* we combine these two clues to realize that the King is in the immediate presence of his future loved one, though she has not yet appeared.

When the ghost appears in *Hamlet*, needless to say, we are aware that the audience is being told to register some form of terror. This would be natural with the arrival of any ghost and beyond that subjectively concerned with the spectator's own attitude towards his father, beginning with the common belief that any returning of the dead is at the very least a great inconvenience. But the Sanskrit theory demands a more formalized reaction from the audience and goes to much greater depths of subtlety. What is left over—the impressionistic, subjective part or the individualized audience reaction—that it may be ineffable, is certainly less significant.

The theory of *rasa* might profitably be employed to investigate some Western dramas—Shakespeare's in particular—and might be experimented with for the Noh play. Western critics have generally dealt with the structure of the action, the arrangement of symbols, or the interactions of clusters of images. They have been suspicious of audience-oriented theories in the light of the "affective fallacy". Insofar as the emotions of the play must be determined by measuring audience reaction, Wimsatt and Beardsley appear to present formidable arguments. But insofar as we are informed in the text or by an actor using a conventional vocabulary of gestures that a certain emotion is the only proper emotion, we are dealing with an element of play structure. This is based, to be sure, on an affective theory but does not depend on the subjective reactions of spectators.

It may be argued, of course, that the dramatic techniques described here are gross elements and not very meaningful, but the point is that they are determinable. Whether we could extend the theory of *rasa* to Western drama in general is another question. We lack, or do not believe, in classifications of the emotions such as we get in the *Dasharupa* but this would seem to be more of a defect in our theory than a criticism of *rasa* theory.[9]

As a course of action, some interdisciplinary conferences should be held—focused on single but broad problems, limited to a dozen or so specialists, and preferably scheduled in such retreats as Airlie or Gould House, or perhaps Princeton on a Sunday, where there is little temptation to do anything but work. The conferences which have accomplished so much for Confucian studies and the very stimulating one held at Indiana University in 1960 on "Style in Language" provide models.

Since it is not likely that the high-level specialist who must attend such conferences if they are to be successful can himself abandon his current research and plunge into new directions in comparative literature, the conferences would attempt to make definitions, point to new areas of research with particular regard to their feasibility, and provide guidelines for projects to be done by graduate students and younger scholars. Various topics have already been suggested—poetics and literary theory, dramatic theory, concepts of periodization in literary history, tradition and revolt, and so on.

It needs to be emphasized, however, that an absolute criterion for useful comparative research is that the basic scholarship for the two components to be compared be both broad and solid. The furthering of basic research in the minor literatures of the world or in minor aspects of the major literatures, though essential does not concern us here. Some areas of Asian literature are well researched: certain major poets in Arabic, Persian, Chinese, and Japanese, certain kinds of poetry in Sanskrit; the Noh and the Kabuki drama; the Sanskrit drama, perhaps the kind of prose narrative represented by the *monogatari*; the epic in the Near East and India. But perhaps not yet so well researched are topics like the great Chinese *Book of Odes* or the variations of the Ramayana in the modern languages of India or its migrations outside continental India. Modern literature presents a rich field, but again the picture is clearest in Japan, where both the literature and the criticism of it is accessible and ancillary sociological data can be found. It is not so easy to comprehend in India or China. In any case, the quantity and quality of available research is a first consideration.

Notes

1. Rene Wellek and Austin Warren, *Theory of Literature*, 3rd ed., 1956, p. 46ff. For discussions of the theory of comparative literature, see its bibliography, pp. 324-26, and Rene Wellek, "The Concept of Comparative Literature", *Yearbook of Comparative Literature*, 2 (1953), 1-5 and his "The Crisis of Comparative Literature," *Comparative Literature : Proceedings of the Second International Congress of Comparative Literature,* ed., W.P. Friederich, 1959, I, 149-59 ; Henry H. H. Remak, "Comparative Literature, Its Definition and Function," *Comparative Literature Method and Prospective*, ed., Newton P. Stallknecht and Horst Frenz, 1961, pp. 3-37 (includes annotated bibliography). For the kinds of and scope of investigations done under the rubric of "comparative literature" see Werner P. Friederich, *Outline of Comparative Literature*, 1954.

2. *Europäische Literatur und Lateinisches Mittelalter,* 1948 ; English translation, 1953.
3. *Mimesis : Dargestellte Wirklichkeit in der Abendländischen Literatur,* Bern, 1946 ; English translation 1953.
4. 1957.
5. 1954 (first published 1949).
6. 1961.
7. 1957.
8. Reprinted in *The Verbal Icon : Studies in the Meaning of Poetry,* 1954, p. 21.
9. Attempts to systematize stage gestures, facial expressions, etc. are not unknown in the West, of course. The eighteenth-century English actor Thomas Betterton (if the ideas are actually his) demonstrates this in the *Life of Thomas Betterton* (1710). The larger topic, the boundary between what common consensus in the West would establish as the chief emotion of an act or scene and the inner world of personal reaction is wide and ill-explored, yet we would all agree that some personal emotions would be clearly in error—the result of misunderstanding, inattention, or psychological blocks.

Comparative Mythology as an Introduction to Cross-Cultural Studies

JOSEPH CAMPBELL*

In teaching women, one is confronted with different sets of academic demands from those of men. Whereas men generally are preparing for specialized careers, the demands of which determine the order and organization of their studies, women are comparatively free to follow the lead of their own interests. In a women's college (at least, of the kind in which I have been teaching), there is, so to say, an open-field situation. We *do not* have required courses; nor do we have examinations. On the other hand, we *do* have a strict and very demanding system of education by dialogue and discussion. I see every one of my students individually, in conferences, for at least one half-hour every fortnight. This makes it possible to follow the growth, direction, and dynamics of each student's individual development.

The instructor in such a situation has to be willing not only to give generously of his time but also to participate in the student's discovery of interests—even to the point, on occasion, of abandoning his own academic plans and point of view. It was in such a fluid environment as this, then, that the course I am going to describe came into being—in relation to a context of interests not primarily academic but experimental.

During my first two or three years, I taught a survey course in comparative literature, but at the close of the second year, three students came to me, separately, to ask for a course in mythology. Apparently my interest in this subject had become more evident in my teaching than I had supposed. I was excited by the idea and decided to give three separate courses—one to each—the following year, based on three quite different reading lists from three different approaches.

At the end of that year, four students came to me for such a course. I brought them together in one class-room, basing the readings and approach that year on what I had learned the year before. Then the year following, there were seven; and from that time on, this course has been both an established part of our curriculum and one of the great joys of my life. I have given up teaching anything else, and since about 1939, have been busily trimming it here, expanding it there, and keeping it up to date.

*Professor Joseph Campbell is a member of the literature faculty of Sarah Lawrence College. He is the author of a *Skeleton Key to Finnegans Wake* (with Henry Morton Robinson), *The Hero With A Thousand Faces*, *The Masks of God*, and editor of Heinrich Zimmer posthuma.

The departmental organization of Sarah Lawrence College is somewhat atypical. We do not have strictly separated departments. There is a literature and language faculty, which is the group with which I am officially associated. Since Sarah Lawrence students have generally professed great interest in the arts, we have strong departments in the fields of dance, theater, music, painting, and sculpture. There is, of course, a large and rather aggressive department in social science, which includes, for some reason or other, philosophy. Psychology is strong and important at Sarah Lawrence—particularly in relation to a greatly appreciated nursery school. And finally, there is a faculty of mathematics and natural science.

In describing this course, I shall be dealing with something out of an age that is long past. Yet my observations about this course—antecedent and indifferent as it is to all academic departmentalization—may be of some use, after all even to those faced with the problems of an elaborately structured university.

The course is conducted in lectures. About 50 per cent of each student's reading is directly related to the topics of the lectures. Each, however, meets me in conference at least once a fortnight, and for these meetings she reads according to her own special interest in whatever direction she has chosen to go. During the first month or so, about half the class will be at a loss. The other 50 per cent, however, will know very well what they want to do and will be off with the gun. As the year proceeds, the others gradually find their bearings.

The individual projects often are developed in relation to some aspect or other of another course, for the material can be approached from many points of view—literary, anthropological, psychological, religious. The course has served, in fact, as an effective coordinating aid for many students. And on the other hand, for those already strongly directed, there is plenty of occasion for more specialized study. I can report that a good many really impressive productions have come onto my desk. One of the most recent is now a beautiful book, Olivia Vlahos, *Human Beginning*, Viking Press, 1966.

The readings for the class begin with Ovid's *Metamorphoses*. Most students think of mythology as classical mythology, and so it has seemed to me that the logical field for a beginning would be here. Besides, Ovid's style is fluent and delightful—not a boring line in the book. The index to the volume, furthermore, provides as good a guide to classical myths as a beginner could require. But the main value of the work, from my point of view, derives from the fact that Ovid grouped his tales in clusters according to theme, so that the student sees immediately how one essential plot can be told and retold with a variety of turns and ascribed to many different heroes. Certain patterns, certain principles, a morphology, can be recognized—the kind of situation that I have expounded in my *Hero with a Thousand Faces*. There is a general pattern to the hero journey—the quest of the hero into unknown realms, the powers that he meets there and overcomes, the stages of his crises of victory, and his return then, with some boon that he has gained, for the founding of a city, religion, dynasty, or what not; or, on the other hand, his failure and destruction. Also in Ovid, right at the begining, parallels with the *Book of Genesis* are evident in the formation of the world, creation of man, the flood, in restoration of the earth, and so on.

Next, after Ovid has set us right in the middle of our subject, we go back to the *Odyssey*, as a great example and test case of what we have learned about the archetypal hero journey. And we are now being introduced, as well, to the historical backgrounds of the classical tradition. After that, we go back one great step further, with Frazer's *Golden Bough*, to pre-Hellenic times.

Frazer is considered by some to be a bit old-fashioned today. At the same time, I do not know of a better way to introduce a completely unprepared student to the whole range of this immense field—its relation to the folk as well as high traditions, the Orient and the Occident, Africa and the Arctic, the great and the little rituals; fairy tales, and all. The same motifs that have already been recognized in the classical field are here revealed as spread throughout the world, the motifs and themes of quest and return, death and rebirth, creation of the world and dissolution. Frazer deals with these in terms largely of their relationship to fertility cults, but he also gives enough material to show their relationship both to cosmological imagery and to the spiritual themes of inward quest, interior sacrifice, and the fertilization of the spirit.

Following Frazer, I used to embark on a review and disscussion of theories—Tylor, Müller, Durkheim, Radcliffe-Brown, and others. After a number of years of this, however, I gave up stressing theory and began to concentrate upon direct presentations of the various mythological traditions themselves, starting with a brief review of some primitive cultures.

I like to classify primitive mythologies in two great categories. In the first are the mythologies of peoples who live and hunt on the great animal plains, where the basic food supply is animal meat and the chief suppliers of the food are men. Most of the hunting tribes inhabit (or once inhabited) the North and South temperate zones. The second category, in direct contrast, comprises the mythologies of peoples of the tropical equatorial belt, whose environment is a steaming jungle and where the chief food supply is vegetable, the women do nearly all the work, and the men devote themselves mainly to their leisure. I think it was Pater Wilhelm Schmidt who, in his *Ursprung der Gottesidee*, first brought out this contrast of the roles of the male in societies, respectively, of the hunt and of the plant world. In the latter, as he says, the primary work is accomplished by the women, who bring forth children, tend the little gardens, build the houses, and take care of them—a fine situation for establishing a profound sense of inferiority in the male.

But the masculine ego, pushed back on itself, responds with that wonderful invention, the men's secret society, where no women are allowed. And there very important things are done. In Melanesia, for example, the major occupation is the raising of pigs—male pigs, of course. The upper canine teeth are knocked out so that the lower tusks can flourish, and they do grow in a beautiful curve, outward and downward and around back through the jaw. The owner of the pig celebrates certain stages of this progress by sacrificing hundreds of other porkers. And if he can get his main pig's tusks to loop around through the jaw and out again, three times, he enjoys all the prestige of a thirty-second degree mason, entitled to such names as "He who walks above the clouds." This is a matter of great psychic importance, because when the man who has raised such a pig dies, he can present it as an offering, instead of himself, to be consumed by Sev Sev, the female guardian of fhe fiery way to the labyrinth of the under-world and immortality.

The survey of these primitive provinces actually starts with examples of mythology from the northern hunting peoples—North Siberian, Eskimo, and American Indian. Then, in America we confront the problem of the tropical planters and the interesting, sensitive question of possible trans-Pacific influence. American anthropologists are not as touchy on this point now as they used to be. I used to regard them as afflicted with a kind of Oedipus complex—not wishing to believe that their motherland, America, might have been fertilized by a foreign intrusion. The amount of passion that this question can generate has always amazed me. I try to be non-committal, but it is difficult not to draw conclusions from the fact that one detail after another of the Middle American cultures has counterparts on the Asian side. After a skirmish with this problem, we return to the Old World by way of the Pacific (Polynesia, Melanesia, the Andamans, and on to Africa). And this concludes the introductory, first portion of the course, the principal aims of which have been to acquaint the student with the most common themes and patterns of world mythology, the geography of the subject, and the modes of inflection of the common themes on the primitive, non-literate level of culture.

The next step is to examine more closely this universality of themes, first in psychological terms. Here we begin with Freud; and since Freud's anthropologist was Frazer, an easy connection can be made with points already noted. To begin with, Frazer's conception of sympathetic magic as based on an association of ideas is not very different from Freud's. Freud simply adds the dimension of associations that are unconscious, a depth of unsuspected layers of association. The student here begins to acquire a new sense, at once of the multi-layered language of myth and of its psychological force. Both Frazer and Freud offer a psychological answer to the problem of the universality of mythic themes. The human psyche everywhere is essentially the same and, responding to essentially the same stimuli, renders patterns of association in fantasy and acts that are also essentially the same.

From Freud the course moves to Jung. Personally, I find Jung as an interpreter of myths far more impressive than Freud. Freud projects a Viennese family romance of Papa, Mama, and their boy-child, into every mythology on earth, regarding myths not as symbolic of adult insights, but as symptomatic of an infantile pathology; regressive, pointing back to childhood. Jung's view, on the other hand, is that the figurations of myths are to be read as the metaphors of a necessary pedagogical discipline, through which the powers of the psyche are led forward to mature relationships, first to the responsibilities of adulthood and then to the wisdom of age.

We spend something like six weeks on Freud and Jung and then move on to the Orient, for which Jung's psychology has already prepared the way. In his introductions to the Tibetan *Book of the Dead* and the Chinese *Secret of the Golden Flower,* he discusses both the similarities and differences between a Western, psychological, scientific approach to mythology and the Oriental, mystical, and devotional. When we have clarified these points, I leave psychology behind and devote the next portion of our years' work to a descriptive historical study of the mythologies of the higher cultures.

These are separated into two great groups with the dividing line at Iran. Westward of this cultural watershed are the two Provinces of Europe and the Levant; eastward, India and the Far East. In both of the oriental provinces the essential belief concerning the ultimate truth, the ultimate substance, the ultimate mystery of being, is that it transcends all description, all naming, and all categories—which is a point not easy for our students to grasp and yet essential to an understanding of Oriental psychology as well as religion.

It is not easy for students to realize that to ask, as they often do, whether God exists and is merciful, just, good, or wrathful, is simply to projectan thropomorphic concepts into a sphere to which they do not pertain. As the Upanishads declare: "There, words do not reach." Such queries fall short of the question. And yet—as the student must also understand—although that mystery is regarded in the Orient as transcendent of all thought and naming, it is also to be recognized as the reality of one's own being and mystery. That which is transcendent is also immanent. And the ultimate function of Oriental myths, philosophies, and social forms, therefore, is to guide the individual to an actual *experience* of his identity with *that; tat tvam asi* ("Thou art that") is the ultimate word in this connection.

By contrast, in the Western sphere—in terms of the orthodox traditions, at any rate, in which our students have been raised—God is a person, the person who has created this world. God and his creation are not of the same substance. Ontologically, they are separate and apart. We, therefore, do not find in the religions of the West, as we do in those of the East, mythologies and cult disciplines devoted to the yielding of an experience of one's *identity* with divinity. That, in fact, is heresy. Our myths and relations are concerned, rather, with establishing and maintaining an experience of *relationship*—and this is quite a different affair. Hence it is, that though the same mythological images can appear in a Western context and an Eastern, it will always be with a totally different sense. This point I regard as fundamental.

In the Orient, the gods do not stand as ultimate terms, ultimate ends, substantial beings, to be sought and regarded in and for themselves. They are more like metaphors, to serve as guides, pointing beyond themselves and leading one to an experience of one's own identity with a mystery that transcends them. I have found that the approach through Freud and Jung greatly helps to make this point clear to students brought up in the mythology of Yahveh—a jealous god, who would hold men to himself and who turned mankind *away* from the Tree of Immortality, instead of leading us to it. Such a god in the Orient would be regarded as a deluding idol. In fact, heaven itself, and our desire for its joys are regarded there as the last barrier, the last obstacle to release, to be transcended. And to escort my students beyond heaven and hell, I take them first to India and then China and Japan.

For India, I begin with a bit of Heinrich Zimmer and Ananda K. Coomaraswamy and go on to the *Upanishads* and the *Gita*. We also read the *Shakuntala* and *Panchatantra*. Buddhism I introduce through Coomaraswamy's *Buddha and the Gospel of Buddhism* and Alan Watts' *The Way of Zen*, with readings in Waley's *Three Ways of Thought in Ancient China* as my introduction to the Far Eastern sphere. Readings are also assigned in Lao-tzu, Confucius, Chuang-tzu, Mencius, and Mo Ti. And then, finally, for Japan, I use Lafacadio Hearn's *Japan*, Okakura Kakuzo's *The Book of Tea*, Herrigel's *Zen in the Art of Archery*, selections form the *Kojiki*, some bits of Noh and Haiku and a lot of enthusiasm of my own.

The course now turns to the West. We have already been introduced to the classical field through Ovid and the *Odyssey*; but I want now to contrast the points of view of Europe and the Levant. It seems to me that where God and Man are viewed as opposed terms, one is inevitably faced with a final decision as to one's ultimate loyalty. Is it to be to God, or is it to be to Man? As I see it, the ultimate loyalty in the Levant has always been to God—in Zoroastrianism, Judaism, Christianity, and Islam. In Europe—whether among the Greeks or Romans, Celts or Germans—it has been to Man.

I see the *Book of Job* as the consummate expression of the Levantine orientation. There, God behaves outrageously—unjustly, unmercifully, brutally and irrationally—yet when Job is confronted with the power and boasting of his tormentor, who now adds insult to injury, he bows in admiration. "Behold," he prays, "I am of small account. I had heard of thee by the hearing of the ear, but now my eyes see thee; therefore I despise myself and repent in dust and ashes."

I contrast with this abdication of human judgment the posture of Prometheus, who was also tortured by a god who could have filled Leviathan's nose with harpoons; and yet, when offered respite if he would but apologize for his aid to man and give honor to that god, he retorted: "I care less than nothing for Zeus; let him do what he likes." I point out to my students that as the ethical humanism of the Greeks developed, their old gods lost stature and force. Their ultimate loyalty was to man. And yet they did not forfeit their primal religious sense of awe before the mystery and wonder of creation. They did not personify that mystery in a being before whom the human spirit should abdicate but, on the contrary, recognized that the supreme manifestation on earth of that same mystery and wonder is the human mind itself, well housed in the beautiful human body.

That is the contrast that I seek to illustrate for my students through the materials of Greece and Rome, the Celts and Germans, the Bible and Islam. And I find that it serves not only to make clear to them certain grand lines of historical stress and conflict, but also to bring out some of the problems of their own lives and beliefs in this strange society of ours, where for six days a week we honor the humanistic values of Greece and Rome and on the seventh for half an hour or so, confess guilt before a jealous Levantine god. Then we wonder why so many of us must repair to the psychoanalyst.

The course comes to a close with a program of medieval and modern readings, dealing in the modern field with two or three authors who have made significant use of mythological forms and themes, such as James Joyce, Thomas Mann, and T.S. Eliot. Through these I can bring Freud, Jung, and the Orient back into our picture again for a culminating summation.

And meanwhile, as already noted, the students have been developing their own projects. For some, the principal interest has been anthropological, through studies of African, Polynesian, Melanesian, or American Indian mythologies. A greatly favored field is Indian mythology and philosophy; another, Buddhism; another, Far Eastern art. In fact, the arts in general are of enormous interest. My wife is a well-known modern dancer, and I always have at least one student who hopes that through my course she may learn to invoke my wife's Muse; Terpsichore, Wagner, and Germanic mythology go together as another favorite topic. Greek drama is still another. Celtic mythology, Arthurian romance, Yeats and the Celtic Twilight authors are always popular ; Dante, Goethe, and Blake, as well : and every year I have two or three students who work through all of Joyce and Thomas Mann. Schopenhauer, Nietzsche, and Jung likewise draw their devotees.

Before the Second World War most of the students who came into the course were of the intellectual type that was generally accused in those days of "ivory tower retreatism." These were young women interested in what I still believe college campuses were made for, namely four years of absorption in science, the liberal arts, and philosophy. Then came the war, Pearl Harbour and all that, and since my course was the only one on the campus at that time that paid any attention whatsoever to the Orient, I suddenly found that my teaching had acquired political importance. This high dignity did not long remain to me, for we now have no end of people who know all about the Orient. And so the course is now again being patronised largely by those interested in philosophy, religion, and the arts. They are so numerous, these days, I am pleased to say, however, that I have had to confine my teaching to seniors, simply to cut down on the number of applicants for admission.

The interest in Oriental art and thought is particularly strong. The interest in Jung is also on the rise. For some reason that I have not been able to determine, the psychologists on our campus have never dealt with Jung. It has always been with Freud, and if Jung's name has been mentioned, it has been only to be misinterpreted and disparaged. And so, it is to my course that students come to be introduced to Jung. The Bible also has become, in late years, a subject of the greatest interest. Every year, I now have two or three going through, from beginning to end, with the *Dartmouth Bible* as guide.

About ten years ago, I was invited to lecture for the State Department at the Foreign Service Institute in Washington, where I was able to test out some of the lessons that I have learned from my young women. What I found was that the same approach works with State Department officers and military men (through Freud and Jung to Oriental mythology, and through mythology to an understanding of the root and commitments of alien culture provinces). And then again, at the Cooper Union in New York, I had the privilege of presenting my entire course to people of still another type, for the most part, moderately educated people, simple and direct, who just wanted to learn. They were not scholars—just curious. And here again, the approach succeeded. Then finally, three years ago, I was invited to deliver a series of lectures on educational television, and for that I simply converted this same course into thirty-four half-hour television programs. Once more, the response was amazing. I would not pretend that there was anything of academic worth about such teaching. It did, however, have the value of opening the minds of people who perhaps would never have thought of such things to the meanings of other cultures and to new possibilities of thought and experience for themselves. The letters that came to the television station originated with men and women of the simplest sort, as well as professionals in many fields of learning.

This experience understandably confirms my conviction that, if we would in our academic world get away from specialization and departmentalization, at least in the *introductory* stages of our cross-cultural studies, a great deal would be gained—not only in understanding, but also in the rapidity with which students would find their way into branches of learning of intimate, genuine interest to themselves. I sometimes think of this course of mine, worked out in such close association with students over the past thirty years, as a kind of pilot project. It is a preliminary sketch of something that in a large university, with cooperating scholars from every one of the fields touched upon, might well take shape as a really important educational project.

While the course is now confined to seniors, it could be addressed even more profitably, I believe, to freshmen. I recall that when I entered Dartmouth there was an excellent freshmen course taught in biology. A required course, it opened up every aspect of the field. There is the need today for something comparable in relation to the rapidly increasing number of approaches to culture and cross-cultural study. Comparative mythology, as I have found, supplies an amazingly serviceable vehicle of approach to every possible aspect of this vast sphere.

Some such elementary course in comparative mythology as I have here suggested—conducted, however, by a team of scholar-specialists lecturing in their special fields and separately directing individual student projects—could be put together readily in any one of the major universities. It would serve not only to open to students a view of the whole range of possibilities before them, when they enter as wide-eyed youngsters the enchanted wood of the world's learning, but also to lead them along, through paths of their own choosing, to explorations of its deep groves.

Approaches in the Study of Japan

DONALD SHIVELY*

The disciplinary distribution of area specialists on Japan—and China—is quite different from that of most other non-European areas. There is a much heavier concentration in the humanities against the social sciences, particularly if we include most of the historians in the former category. The numerical superiority of the humanists has shaped the available body of research on Japan, and it will therefore be useful to look briefly at this phenomenon before we pass on to consider the main concern of this paper—namely, the current state of research on Japan from the standpoint of its usefulness to comparative studies.

Actually, the origin of the difference can be simply stated. It relates to the literate cast of the Chinese and Japanese civilizations—the vast corpus of literary and historical records—and the millennial loyalty to this "high tradition." We need also to take into account the significant part long played in Western scholarship by language study of these areas.

It should be understood that Japanese studies before World War II developed in the shadow of Chinese studies particularly the European tradition of Sinology, which, in turn, had been modeled on Greek and Latin studies. Every Sinologist was a textual scholar, a philologist, a translator, an historian. He roamed far and wide, touching on a range of subjects such as philosophy, religion, folklore, mythology, archaeology, and art history. He was an area specialist who, relatively speaking, was better equipped with research tools than with our modern notions of discipline. In the classical traditions, he worked on earlier periods of history.

In the 1930's few young scholars emerged who undertook studies of the history of more recent times, from the medieval period to the nineteenth century, but most commonly the nineteenth century. It was these historians who shaped area studies on East Asia in our universities in the years after 1945. The war with Japan gave the first important impetus to the growth of East Asian studies. Of the several thousand Americans who began the study of Japanese in military programs, several hundred went on to graduate work in Chinese or Japanese studies. The Army Specialized Training Program and other

---

*Donald Shively taught at the University of California, Berkeley, from 1950 to 1962 and at Stanford University from 1962 to 1964 and is presently Professor of Japanese History and Literature at Harvard. He is the author of studies on the social and cultural history of Japan in the seventeenth, eighteenth, and nineteenth centuries.

wartime area programs led directly to the postwar interdisciplinary area programs, which provided the opening for social scientists with a research commitment to China and Japan.

The number of specialists on China and Japan who have been trained in the social sciences is not impressive—the demand far outstrips the supply. Historians still greatly outnumber those of other disciplines. By way of illustration, consider the number of doctorates awarded at Harvard for dissertations on East Asian subjects between 1931 and 1965. Of the 201 Ph. D.'s, 115 were in the field of history (although not all in the history department). This proportion appears to be continuing, for there are currently over 70 graduate students beyond the M.A. level in the East Asian history programs, more than in all other fields of the humanities and social sciences combined. (The appointment recently of several additional social scientists is beginning to affect these proportions at Harvard.) Generally speaking, the situation seems to be similar elsewhere in the United States in East Asian studies, in marked contrast to South Asian, Southeast Asian, and African studies, which are over-balanced the other way.

There are at least two reasons for the continuing perference of graduate students for history. One is the scholarly tradition, mentioned earlier, of studies which have been carried forward by the senior faculty and hence exert influence by example on graduate students. The other is the greater demand, at least in terms of formal degree requirements, imposed on students in the social science departments. The attitude of these departments is that the students are primarily economists, sociologists, or political scientists, for example, and only incidentally are writing their dissertations on an area topic. In other words, they expect the students to be sound in theory and to be competent as generalists—and quite properly, for otherwise the students could not gain recognition within the discipline.

But some departments have been slow to recognize that in order to work on East Asia a lasting area commitment is also necessary. For research on China or Japan, the student needs at least four year-courses in one language. He should have two or three in the other, and then must keep up and improve this competence thereafter. In addition, he must have a wide range of knowledge of the area. The demands on the historian are somewhat less stringent as regards the discipline or department. He is expected to have some competence in one or two Western history areas, but he is not a generalist in the same sense. The theory requirement is usually not very formidable.

Having taken this quick measure of the distribution of scholars on Japan, let us now discuss some of the approaches used in research in the humanities and the social sciences and some of the problems encountered, which will be of interest to the comparativist. On the latter's behalf, it should be pointed out that, despite the disciplinary imbalance (and various factors restricting scholarship on the areas which have not been considered), we are better supplied with data on Japan, and over a wider range of coverage, than on most of the other countries of Asia and Africa. Japan is also a culture that lends itself, with relative facility, to comparisons with Western areas and with some parts of Asia, although this attribute is not without its dangers, as we shall see.

There has been remarkable activity in the study of Japanese literature during the last fifteen years and this, therefore, seems to be an extremely promising field for comparative study. We may mention as of particular interest to students of the literature of many European and Asian countries, the evolution of a variety of major dramatic forms. Among these are the Noh and Kabuki, prose *genre* types quite different from the West or China, the existence of characteristic poetic techniques which have, in some of their forms, made a contribution to French and English poetry, the eleventh century Japanese "novel", and the emergence of the modern novel in this century. Detailed study of texts and analysis of works has been undertaken in a number of doctoral dissertations, occasionally, to be published. The substantial number of translations from Japanese literature has attracted wide attention and has made practicable the inclusion of Japanese literature in "great books" courses and literature surveys. We do not yet have representative coverage, but we have come a long way.

The disappointing aspect, however, is that virtually nothing has been done in research in comparative literature. Some of our leading translators, well grounded in English literature and literary criticism, are capable of undertaking this type of work, but to date they have been more attracted to translating or studying individual authors.

One exceptional work to be noted in passing is *Japanese Court Poetry,* by Robert Brower and Earl Miner,[1] respectively, a specialist on Japanese literature and a scholar of seventeenth century English poetry (who also knows Japanese). While not explicitly comparative, this remarkable collaborative effort is fundamentally comparative in the sense that it analyzes the Japanese poetical tradition by applying, whenever possible, the criteria used in the study of English poetry. The result is not only very different from what we have had from Japanese scholars but also provides us with analytical tools that can be used to compare the Japanese poetic tradition with that of other cultures.

Is it necessary to be a specialist in Japanese literature to use it in comparative work? It has been said that a teacher of English literature is likely to do a better job of presenting the *Tale of Genji* to a class of undergraduates than a Japanese specialist. This may often be the case in an introductory or world literature survey type of course. The outsider's fresher approach and the common bond of English literature with his class may strike a warmer response, at least among undergraduates. But note that what we have here is an *exposure* to works of Japanese literature, not their study.

Again, scholars of Western (or Chinese) literature can make—and have made—a contribution to the understanding of even advanced students and specialists in Japanese literature through the means of insights and analogies which emerge out of their different perspective. Yet here also there are definite limitations. The existing materials in English on the cultural environment and traditions that have helped to form a particular work are either lacking or scarce. A knowledge of Japanese is necessary in a still more crucial sense. A literary work cannot really be judged in any language but its own.

In translation, even the content often comes through in complete or altered form. The translator is generally an advocate of the work he presents, and he is anxious to have it read and appreciated in the West. To achieve maximum acceptability, he takes liberties with the text, which range from transposition and by passing an "unfortunate sentence," to leaving out long passages judged to be difficult or uninteresting for the Western reader (such as accounts of ceremonials). In Arthur Waley's otherwise admirable version of the *Tale of Genji*[2] some of these omissions run to many pages. Today's translators are generally not so bold as Waley, but they do take liberties to make the translation "come off" better.

These procedures are defensible when the translations are without scholarly pretensions and are intended for general reading. But the user of the translation whose interest is comparative literature should be aware that he has in hand not the work itself, but a less than faithful translation—and certainly less faithful than those rendered of European literature. This warning must be repeated for the historian or social scientist who turns to translation of literature in his search for concrete expressions of the psychology, mores, value system, or "style" of a foreign culture. The things that are not translated, or that are handled differently, are of course those which are often most alien to our tradition and which are therefore particularly significant.

In many significant areas of the humanities, the scholarly study of Japan is just beginning. We may single out art, music, theater, religion and philosophy, which are represented by only very small numbers of truly qualified specialists. We find solid articles and monographs, but the base is narrow. There is a dearth of reliable surveys. Although all these fields offer attractive subjects for comparative analysis, particularly with China, there has not yet been enough study in depth in either country to make possible comparisons except on a rather elementary level. How interesting these could be is evident from de Bary's "Some Common Tendencies in Neo-Confucianism."[3] Yet much progress has been made in the last fifteen years; the advance of each new monograph is welcome and often represents a substantial achievement.

In contrast to other branches of the humanities, historians have long had a penchant for comparisons, although many of the works of the older tradition hardly come under the heading of "comparative studies." Indeed, Japan, seems to have tempted irresistibly. In speaking of James Murdoch's pioneer three volume *History of Japan* (1903-1922), Sir George Sansom said:

> It is marred by a dreadful facetiousness and a habit of introducing such maddening analogies as a "Japanese Jerusalem" a 'Japanese Agnes of Dunbar,' and even 'Japanese Cornishmen'. These faults bring the writer's judgement under suspicion, while it is clear that his aesthetic sense was but feebly developed. It might be said that he presented Japan as seen through spectacles made in Aberdeen about 1880."[4]

While Murdoch's degree of ethnocentricity is unusual, historians in general have not always eschewed judgments based on Western values, institutional analysis framed in terms of apparent European equivalents, or an exaggeration of the pervasiveness of foreign influence (significant though this was). Whatever the ground chosen, a comparative analysis must be rooted first, in the Japanese experience. It is only after we have tried to view the history of Japan from the inside, as it were, that we can begin to make systematic comparisons with aspects of non-Japanese civilizations.

One example of the kind of enticement we have been talking about is that produced by Japanese feudalism. There was the following sequence of conditions in Japan: the decline in authority of the imperial government, the emergence of a manorial system, a local military class, a loyalty ethic, the breakdown of the manorial system and the development of territorially united fiefs. Stated in these terms, the parallel with European feudalism seems obvious. And indeed it is close. But there are interesting differences of detail, many of which have not yet been fully explored. The various steps in this classic sequence have still to be measured carefully. We may find that in carrying to Japan the words "imperial", "manor", "loyalty", and "fief", we have brought with them undeclared items of European culture. Intrinsic dissimilarities of function are obscured. (A *comparative* study can become a contrastive study, as more detail is called into play. The required level of specificity—or generality—will determine the issue.)

The first noteworthy contribution to the comparative study of Japanese feudalism was made fifty years ago, by Asakawa at Yale; he took as his standards French and German feudalism. Other important works are Reischauer's chapter on Japan in Coulborn's *Feudalism in History*[5] and Jouon des Longrais' *L' Est et L'Ouest: Institutions du Japon et de L' Occident Comparees*.[6] 'Particularly valuable for comparative' purposes is an article by J. W. Hall, "Feudalism in Japan—A Reassessment"[7] in which he points out that the acceptance of Western European and Japanese feudalism as two relatively similar models has prepared the way for the next stage in the analysis, to determine which elements were critical and which fortuitous in creating the parallel.

There are other phenomena in Japanese history which distinguish it from its Asian neighbors and point to comparisons with Western Europe, such as the development of semi-autonomous, commercial cities (although short-lived), in the sixteenth century and the rise of bourgeous culture in the seventeenth century. More recent additions include the high literacy rate as a pre-industrial development, and the Germanic configuration of the Meiji state, with its militarism and totalitarianism. The present generation of historians, as Hall said, "has begun to view Japanese history, not merely as something unique in itself but as a subject which, when combined with the data of European history provides a broader basis for the testing of general concepts of institutional change or other social theories."[8]

A recent contribution along these lines is represented by a series of six conferences on the modernization of Japan with participants from different disciplines. In the first conference volume, *Changing Japanese Attitudes Toward Modernization*,[9] there are a number of papers with comparative dimensions: Hall's on concepts of modernization, Dore's on what education meant in Japan as compared to England, Craig's on science and Confucianism in Japan with contrasts for China, Passin's on Japanese intellectuals with comparisons to India and elsewhere, and also two contrastive papers on China and India by specialists on those areas. The study of Japan's modernization seems to point to Europe for comparisons but to China and other countries of Asia for contrasts.

China was the source of much of Japan's higher culture—Buddhism, Confucianism, the writing system, two-thirds of the vocabulary, the structure of the Imperial court and government, and most of the arts. Yet there have always been striking differences in the development of the two countries, most recently in the contrast between China's slow rate of modernization and Japan's position as a world power by 1905 and its status as the world's fourth industrial power today.

Of the multiple differences, between Japan and China in the 1870's which were the crucial ones in determining the differing rate of development? There is probably speculation on this question in every lecture course on the modern Far East in this country, but very few have attempted to formulate this complex problem in writing. Marion Levy paid particular attention to the differences in social structure in "Contrasting Factors in the Modernization of China and Japan."[10] Reischauer has suggested that the feudal experience in Japan, "which so closely paralleled that of Europe, may have had something to do with the speed and ease with which the Japanese during the past century refashioned their society on European models." He indicates that such factors in Japanese society as the aristocratic military tradition, the code of honor, national consciousness, concepts of law, styles of economic and social organization (all of which can be contrasted with Chinese institutions) may well have accounted for Japan's early lead in modernization.[11] Still other factors which have been suggested in this respect are the Japanese interest in scientific discovery in the pre-industrial period and the high rate of literacy.

It is not surprising that the interests of historians of both China and Japan have clustered on the late nineteenth century and the opening of the twentieth century. These were times of complex change, when pressure from the West triggered internal reform, modern nationalism, and programs of modernization. As developments in each country are better understood, we shall be acquiring material for interesting comparative work. (The "bunching" of historians on this period has entailed some losses. While promising for the study of modernization, one consequence is the restricted attention given to other periods of Japanese history).

In the social sciences, as I indicated at the outset of this paper, the volume of research on comparative problems lags behind that done in the humanities. In two recent textbooks, political scientists have successfully presented the material on Japan with a view to its use comparatively. In *Major Governments of Asia*[12] the country chapters are similar in structure to facilitate comparisons by the reader.

Modern Political Systems: Asia,[13] uses a somewhat more structured approach aimed at the comparison of political systems. As the coverage devoted to Japan is necessarily limited in these books, totalling about 100 pages in each, the discussion is correspondingly general.

Other comparative work is reported in *Political Modernization in Japan and Turkey*[14] which brings together the papers presented at a conference held by the Social Science Research Council Committee on Comparative Politics. These two countries appear to reflect suggestive parallels: Asian countries of the same language family (although distant cousins), "backward" when the threat from the West spurred modernization as a defensive reaction, and, unlike most Asian countries, independent throughout their history. But the parallel does not go very far. Wide differences separate the other pre-existing conditions and, with such a large number of variables, the critical ones are difficult to identify.

The detailed research on the Japanese government is slowly pushing forward in the hands of a few scholars. Important work has been done on constitutions, political parties, and voting patterns and local government in a few areas. As yet little attention has been given to the role of mass media, education, student movements, and labor or to the study of bureaucracy and political elites.

In the other social sciences, research on Japan has had an even later start. Since both the approach and the data are new, this work is of particular interest for comparative studies.

Social anthropologists have added half a dozen village studies to the single example that existed before the war. There have also been valuable studies of kinship terminology and family structure, which invite comparisons with China and other societies.

In sociology, Max Weber's study of the secular repercussion of different religious doctrines in Europe and China provides points of reference for Robert Bellah's *Tokugawa Religion*[15] Ezra Vogel's earlier research on the working class of South Boston gives a comparative dimension to his recent book, *Japan's New Middle Class*.[16] Only during the last few years have we had studies by psychologists who know Japanese and have done fieldwork in Japan. Experimentation in the application of Freudian categories to Japanese society is reported in George De Vos' articles on psychological testing of delinquents and other subjects. William Caudill's work on value orientation and Robert Lifton's psychological studies of both Chinese and Japanese youth are making available comparative data in this area for the first time.

Although there are very few economists who specialize on Japan, some excellent studies have been produced. William Lockwood's extensive studies of Japanese industrialization are pertinent as he is concerned with the differing rates and patterns of industrial development in Japan, China, and India. One of the most successful examples of the use of the comparative method is the fourth chapter of Henry Rosovsky's *Capital Formation in Japan 1868-1940*.[17] He analyzes Japanese economic development over the last century against an idealized Western pattern, the Gerschenkron Model, which deals with the economic growth of France, Germany, and Russia. He pays particular attention to Gerschenkron's special sequence for Russia, as the most backward of these three European countries. Broadly speaking, there is enough similarity between the development of Japan and the model, used that the exposure brings into relief many peculiarities of the Japanese experience. Singling out the typical features in Japan's pre-industrial baseline, he describes them in historical depth and goes on to compare the quality of Japan's industrial development with a wide range of Western countries.

Like the historians, some social scientists have been fascinated with the Japanese-German modernization parallel. Two suggestive papers published recently are, in both instances, by scholars whose previous work had been entirely on Western areas. Reinhard Bendix's "Preconditions of Development:

A comparison of Japan and Germany"[18] approaches these countries on the eve of modernization and focuses primarily on the ideological articulations of the aristocracy, examining the latter's relationship to the land, its traditions as ruling class, and so on. "Japan and Europe : Contrasts in Industrialization"[19] by David S. Landes, considers some major conditions bearing on industrial development, such as the political challenge, reform, leadership, the role of the agrarian sector, and the side-effects of high-pressure industrialization.

Both papers stand as good examples of the effectiveness of the comparative approach. Both also demonstrate that the generalist or the specialist from another geographical area can be very instructive to the Asian fields when he does some serious digging.

In conclusion, let us consider what the foregoing discussion suggests about comparative courses for undergraduates. The sketch of the present state of Japanese studies offered here indicates that in all the disciplines we do not have nearly so solid a foundation of detailed or monographic research as in European studies and that we are, therefore, not standing on grounds of equal reliability. The disparity is even greater in the case of most other countries of Asia and Africa. We all recognize that it is essential, nonetheless, to give more attention to non-Western areas in the curriculum. Comparative courses are one way to achieve this aim, and probably the way to reach the largest proportion of undergraduates.

Trial efforts with comparative courses should be encouraged, provided that it is recognized (and freely admitted) that the non-Western materials now available are sometimes fragmentary and unreliable. They represent a pioneering stage in scholarship. A questioning attitude should be the rule here. The fundamental propositions should be questioned and alternative interpretations considered to a greater extent than is usual with the handling of more familiar areas.

Far from being incompatible, comparative studies and area studies should work together to offset each other's hazards and limitations. The danger for those taking the area studies approach, whether researchers of faculty and undergraduates, is that implicit for all specialists of viewing the subject too narrowly or not seeing it in relation to other areas. The comparative approach helps to protect against this.

The weakness of comparative courses, on the other hand, is that limited time permits the presentation of only highly selective and easily definable phenomena in the two or more cultures involved in the comparison. This results in a high degree of generalization, with minimal attention to the historical traditions and cultural environment which helped shape the phenomena under study. The comparativist will benefit from having at this institution some area specialists to serve as resources for him, to make available "analyses in depth" in at least one of the non-Western areas covered in comparative courses. In short, comparative and area specialists need each other, not only in research, but also in teaching.

Every college and university should, in time, have at least one program on a non-Western region. Simply the presence of such a program on the campus affects the world view of all students at the institution, even those who do not enroll in it. Area studies are expensive to mount, as they should include language courses, area specialists in several disciplines, and a library collection in both Western languages and the language of the area. To begin with, most colleges should not undertake a program on more than one Asian or African area, and universities should also be prudent about the number of areas to which they make a commitment. There have been cases of areas centers proliferating at universities, with consequent shortages both of qualified personnel and funds. The result has been inadequate performance in instruction and research.

Both comparative and area courses should be thought of as general education. They should not become a nucleus for majors in the undergraduate curriculum, although either might serve as a minor, the major being in a traditional discipline. Even such a minor, whether in a non-Western area or comparative field, would not be my choice for an undergraduate who plans to do graduate work and train himself for a scholarly career in one of the area fields. He should have a broad education in Western civilization and strength in a specific discipline which would be sacrificed if he were to specialize prematurely.

In practice, of course, a career decision to go into area studies is rarely made by a college freshman. This is no doubt just as well, for it removes the hazard of having his choice master-minded by one of us in possession of what he thinks is the best formula. Educational goals are, of course, highly individual matters. In spite of bad advice or poor instruction or premature specialization, the good mind will educate itself. But good results might be achieved earlier if the student's undergraduate major were in the discipline that he would later follow in area specialization, or even in another related discipline or in some way contributing to his eventual choice of specialization.

The preceding applies particularly to the social sciences, but in the humanities, where "discipline" means something less specific, one or two recommendations are possible, based on the significance attached to a good grounding in methodology. For the would-be historian of Japan, a major in European history, with special attention to the middle ages or, perhaps, the classical period, would be useful. For students of Japanese literature, a good foundation can be gained from Greek and Latin, English, or comparative literature. It is desirable, when possible, to begin language training as an undergraduate and possibly in secondary school.

But how do we lure students into non-Western studies or interest them in studying one of the non-Western languages? Our best devices are undoubtedly the area and comparative study courses considered earlier in this discussion, notwithstanding the problems and limitations of such courses.

Notes

1. Robert Brower and Earl Miner, *Japanese Court Poetry*, 1961.

2. Murasaki Shikibu, *A Tale of Genji*, tr. by Arthur Waley, 1935.

3. In D. S. Nivison and A. F. Wright, *Confucianism in Action*, 1959.

4. *Japan : A Short Cultural History*, 1938, p. 519.

5. 1956.

6. 1958.

7. *Comparative Studies in Society and History,* October, 1962, pp. 15-51,

8. *Japanese History : New Dimensions of Approach and Understanding,* Publication No. 34, Service Center for Teachers of History, 1961.

9. Marius Jansen, ed., *Changing Japanese Attitudes toward Modernization,* 1965.

10. S.E. Kuznets et al, ed., *Economic Growth: Brazil, India, Japan,* 1955.

11. R. Coulborn, ed., *Feudalism in History,* 1956, pp. 46-47, and cited by Hall in "Feudalism in Japan," p. 51.

12. George T. McKahin, ed., *Major Government of Asia,* 1963.

13. R.E. Ward and R.C. Macridis, eds., *Modern Political Systems: Asia*, 1963.

14. R.E. Ward and D.A. Rustow, eds., *Political Modernization in Japan and Turkey*, 1964.

15. 1957.

16. 1963.

17. 1961.

18. *Nation-Building and Citizenship*, 1964, pp. 177-213.

19. W.W Lockwood, ed., *The State and Economic Enterprise in Japan*, 1965, pp. 93-182.

Comparative Studies in Undergraduate Education

WM. THEODORE de BARY*

Any exploration of the relation between Asian studies and comparative studies must immediately confront the question of what the term "Comparative studies" means. Comparative studies of what? All studies are basically comparative. In the sciences, one compares different bodies of data in order to identify regularities among them. In the humanities one compares different forms of experience with each other and especially with one's own. The striving for universality in all branches of learning compels the widest possible comparison.

But if the word "comparative" is not simply a redundancy in the present context, its significance must be bound up with efforts to encourage "non-Western" studies, which has been a continuing, and much-discussed movement in American education in recent years. There is a feeling, apparently, that both scholarship and education still suffer from an imbalance between the intensive and extensive exploration of the world we live in, and more particularly that in the social sciences and humanities a pre-occupation with the limited experience of Western man has prevented us from sharing fully in the experience of other peoples.

It would be a large order to take up the question, "What can comparative studies of Asia contribute to extending the frontiers of knowledge in the various disciplines?" This discussion, therefore, concentrates on the more manageable problem of the relation of comparative studies of Asia to undergraduate education. Consequently, in what follows I speak not as a specialist in Neo-Confucianism but as one who represents the common discipline of teaching, especially on the undergraduate level. Neo-Confucianism, in my judgment, is an important and fruitful subject of comparative study, involving Japan and Korea as well as China and involving also the larger problem of the "modernization" of traditional societies. But my experience as a teacher, as well as my awareness of the challenge which comparative studies of Neo-Confucianism represent for even advanced scholars, suggests that this is a kind of study which few undergraduates could hope to do research in, though its larger implications are certainly relevant to even an introductory course on East Asia.

---

*Wm. Theodore de Bary is Chairman of the Department of Chinese and Japanese, Chairman of the Committee on Oriental Studies, and Director of the East Asian Language and Area Center of Columbia University. He is co-author and editor of *Approaches to the Oriental Classics* and *Approaches to Asian Civlizations*.

It should be made clear at the outset that in my own order of priorities for undergraduate education, I put what is conventionally known as area studies rather far down the list. It is something for the success of which other studies are a prerequisite. On the other hand, comparative studies in some shape or sense seems to me involved in the educational process almost from the beginning. As I have explained elsewhere in discussing the relation of language and area studies to undergraduate education, area studies (meaning a broad, multi-disciplinary approach to a given area, combined with competence in the language (s) of that area) must yield precedence to both liberal education, and the necessary disciplinary training.[1]

It is my assumption that any college which aims at a genuinely liberal education, or calls itself a "liberal arts college," must devote a substantial part of the first two years to general education or a core curriculum of some sort. I assume, too, that because it is so important to get an early start on difficult Asian languages, whatever time can be spared from general education in the first two years can easily be taken up by beginning language study. Finally I think we can assume today that educators and employers no longer have much use for the kind of area trainee who has substituted area coverage for disciplinary specialization. The student must rather have competence in a discipline which he can then bring to the study of an area.

It is unrealistic to think that, in his junior and senior years, the student can both ground himself in a given discipline, like history, anthropology, government or economics, and also follow an inter-disciplinary program that covers his area from every angle. Compelled to opt for one or the other, we can only choose the former. We must be satisfied if on graduation from college the student has received a general introduction to the area, a basic discipline that he can work in, and a command of the language appropriate to his discipline. A more comprehensive knowledge of the area will have to wait, either upon practical experience in the field or upon an interdisciplinary regional studies program on the M.A. level.[2]

If these things are true, then we must clearly distinguish the different needs of the student on the successive levels of education. We must likewise consider the value of comparative studies, not only in relation to the overall aims of scholarship but also in relation to the their suitability and feasibility at each stage of the educational process. Hence we need to define the problem at each level, if we are not to work at cross-purposes. As the context for my own discussion of comparative studies, therefore, I offer the following educational sequence, for students engaged in Asian studies:

1. General education in the lower college, with an introduction to the major Asian civilizations and Oriental humanities for all students—following the basic Western courses in the second year (or where necessary the third).

2. A major in the upper college emphasizing:

    a. language study begun as early as the students' preparation for college allows, without sacrificing some Western language competence and utilizing summers for intensive study;

    b. initiation into the basic methodology of a discipline or profession;

    c. application of language and discipline to seminar research in the senior year.

3. An inter-disciplinary area study program on the M. A. level, or travel, study, and practical experience in the area. Both will be necessary for most students who look forward to careers as area specialists.

4. Ph. D, work in a given discipline, with all the skills and experience gained thus far brought to focus on a specific topic of research.

It is not difficult to show the exciting intellectual possibilities that can be explored through comparative studies. Nor, on the other hand, can we fail to see what frustration will develop if undergraduates are tempted by the challenge of comparative studies to undertake sophisticated procedures and linguistic skills beyond their means. From my own experience as a teacher I would say that most undergraduates are naturally comparative in their approach. They are fascinated by similarities and differences among civilizations, and imagination helps where knowledge fails, to spin out great theories and systems. The results are sometimes ludicrous, but I see no real harm if the student's passion for construction and coherence is led into disciplined channels.

A great danger, perhaps, lies in a student's being led down such channels without knowing where he started from or why he is there. Within particular disciplines a measure of control, and hence of intellectual security, is provided by the methodology which has been developed to handle the subject matter. This tells us which comparisons are relevant and which irrelevant to the questions at hand. But the tendency of most methodologies is to be analytic—to exclude and to isolate—and the precise definition of relevance can paradoxically reach the point where most of life has been excluded from our inquiry, and our studies lose all relevance to the larger world in which we live. In the end, a synthetic or holistic approach is thus as necessary a complement to disciplinary training as the latter is a necessary refinement of our crude appetite to digest the world.

In this connection, it has been a revelation to me that unexpected benefits are derived from the exposure of highly trained specialists to undergraduate general education courses embracing several Asian civilizations. In quite a few cases these specialists come into the courses after years of specialized doctoral training, which have not been preceded (for want of any such opportunity) by any general course on Asia conceived as part of a liberal education. As teaching assistants, interns, or merely observers, they are challenged by this broadening experience to re-examine their own area of study in the light of other areas. They are not only awakened to other possibilities but see new significance even in their own narrow field when viewed in a comparative light.

This observation, moreover, has been confirmed by contact with young scholars at other institutions. Repeatedly those who showed a capacity to see beyond their own special field of study or viewed their own field in a larger perspective were those who had held teaching assistantships in general introductory courses on Asia.

On the level of general education, the question arises of how comparative such introductory courses can be and in what way. At a conference devoted to "Approaches to Asian Studies," the anthropologist, Francis L. K. Hsu, came out strongly for an explicit comparative approach.

> In Asian studies, there should be two kinds of comparisons, both equally important : (1) for American researchers and teachers, comparison between Japan and the United States, China and the United States, Indonesia and the United States, and the like; and (2) for researchers and teachers in all countries, between Japan and China; Hindu India and Japan ; etc.
>
> These comparisons are necessary for the following reasons : Any student of culture or civilization will make implicit comparisons between the culture he studies and his own culture, whether such a research worker or teacher consciously wishes him to do so or not. Since the researcher or the teacher is, like all human beings, a product of his own culture, with its own particular values, assumptions, and prejudices, it seems imperative that such comparisons, be made on the conscious

rather than the unconscious level....In my view implicit comparison is far more dangerous than explicit comparison. In explicit comparison the student at least puts himself on record, so that he himself can rationally examine the result of his comparison, and others can judge the factual or logical bases of his comparison as well as the merits or the demerits of his comparison....

Many scholars of the Orient have the peculiar view that the societies under their scrutiny are unique or are totally dissimilar to anything that is known in the West. My comment on such a view is that, if we seek differences, no two indviduals are ever identical, but two individuals who are not identical can be compared for their similarities just as much as for their differences. An attempt to compare different phenomena for the common principles and common factors which govern them does not mean the negation of the particular characteristics and unique features which distinguish any one of them. The fire generated on a match is certainly different from the fire radiated from the sun. These two phenomena can nevertheless be compared, and must be compared, at some point of our research on heat....[3]

With these remarks, and others in the same conference too extensive to quote, I largely agree. As a teacher, however, I wonder how far one can go on the introductory level to meet these exact spceifications. In the end this will no doubt depend on how even introductory courses are conceived and planned. But, applying Professor Hsu's two kinds of comparison above, it seems obvious that an introduction to Oriental civilizations must deal with more than one civilization if it is to serve his second objective, i.e., provide comparisons among the Asian civilizations, as well as between any one of them and American civilization.

At Columbia, if we have included the major civilizations of India, China, and Japan in our Oriental civilizations course, it is precisely because they represent a sufficient degree of both unity and diversity to illumine one another. In these relatively well-defined areas we may examine the pervasive problems of the ancient agrarian civilizations, the economic relationships, social arrangements, and political institutions which contributed to the stability and durability of the most mature Oriental civilizations, and then see these alongside the comparatively younger, more dynamic, and less stable society of Japan.

But to present a reasonably well-rounded picture of a civilization, we must draw on the results of various disciplinary approaches, and if the picture is also to be that of a dynamic historical process, rather than of a static cross-section segmented by disciplines, it will always be a question where one can interrupt the process in order to compare explicitly, and with any degree of rigor, similar aspects of two different civilizations. This problem comes up constantly in class because students are so irrepressibly comparative in their thinking.My conviction is that we should want to stimulate this kind of thinking, and be glad that it is spilling out all the time, while recognizing that it is both theoretically and practically impossible to deal with all of the questions thus aroused.

In each such case what intrigues the thinking student is not just a similarity or a difference between two or more civilizations, but a combination of similarites and differences which suggests a greater variety of causal factors in each situation than he had first recognized. Suddenly illuminated, he points out one such factor as explaining the difference. The instructor naturally recognizes this as an over-simplification. There are other factors at work too, some of them not quite so evident in the period under discussion as perhaps in a later phase of the civilization which has yet to be dealt with. The best he can do is to analyze the situation as it lies before the student, emphasize the unknowns that remain to be investigated, and ask that a comparative judgment be suspended until more returns are in. Often, of course, this means a long wait.

Take for example, the role of the middle class in Asian civilizations. The student who has studied either India or China will probably be struck by the relative insignificance of the middle class—its numerically small size, its social inferiority, the subordination of its economic activities to those of the state and agriculture, its lack of political initiative and leadership, and its failure to take a more creative role in culture. As compared to the dynamic role of the middle class in the modern West, this appears to be a significant difference between traditional Asian civilizations and our own. If the student makes this comparison even in rough terms when he encounters the phenomenon in, for example, India, he makes as Professor Hsu says an implicit comparison between the culture he studies and his own. Then, if he goes on to encounter the same phenomenon in China, he will probably be tempted to think that this common feature of the two great Asian civilizations represents a basic difference between East and West.

And he will be wrong, of course, but not terribly wrong (at least no more so than Toynbee and Northrop have been in similar matters). This is indeed a widespread feature of Asian civilizations. But, if the student goes on to study Japan and its historical development, he notices that in the sixteenth and seventeenth centuries a significant middle class begins to develop, which threatens to undermine the economic position of the "feudal" ruling class and which develops a bourgeois life and culture that has since compelled the admiration of the world. At this point the student's earlier judgment must be modified. Somehow, if the growth of a middle class represents a crucial difference to the dynamics of a civilization, Japan must, in terms of his earlier comparison be more "Western" than "Eastern".

Here again, he may be more right than wrong, but the instructor will have to point out the social and political disabilities of the bourgeoisie in Japan of this period and the significant limits on its economic activities imposed by the Tokugawa seclusion policy. It will be a temptation further for the teacher to anticipate later developments and discuss the comparative role of the bourgeoisie in the evolutionary changes of the nineteenth century in Japan and the West, where important differences emerge between the two. And if he does not restrain himself, he can pursue this particular comparison right down to the present, discussing the nature and role of the middle class in the early decades of this century, the heyday of big business, "free" enterprise, and liberal politics, making all the necessary qualifications which the use of these terms require tn the Japanese context. Then the 1930's and the 1940's will have new things to teach about the relative position and leadership potential of the middle class, as will the postwar period in a very different way. Since this is a question which modern Japanese historians have debated continually, one which has important political overtones, and one which sociologists can explore from numerous angles, there is almost no end to what can be done with this question arising in the student's mind.

But the instructor who is lured down this particular path today, and another by-path tomorrow, making the most of each opportunity for comparative examination, may end up giving a very disjointed account of Japanese civilization. What would be quite admissible, if one could assume a basic familiarity with some historical framework, becomes an impossibility for an introductory course. For this reason, the teacher in such a course must constantly restrain himself and his students from plunging headlong into many of the numerous comparative inquiries which the deliberate juxtaposition of ideas, institutions, and historical situations has opened up.

The instructor must accustom the student to living with such questions and rarely getting full answers. For, even if he has asked that a partial answer be accepted for the moment, and a kind of parenthesis be put around it which can be opened later as a fuller picture emerges, he knows full well that there will never be time at the end of the course to deal, individually and exhaustively, with all the questions thus held in abeyance. At least, the most I have ever been able to do is to take a few such comparative problems, analyze them with the students, see how many of the relevant questions could be answered on the basis of their accumulated knowledge, and what kinds of inquiry and evidence would be needed to deal with those that remained. Finally as a test of their skill in handling such problems, I would regularly include questions on the final examination dealing with comparative aspects of these civilizations which we had *not* had time to discuss fully in class—questions such as the comparative role of military elites, political parties, corporate organizations, industrialization programs, nationalism, traditionalist reactions, and so on, in China, Japan, and India. Thus, the comparative aspect of things has never been lost sight of even though I would reject the idea that it is feasible, either intellectually or pedagogically, to undertake the comparative study of civilizations as a whole in such a course.

> In any introduction to Asia, such comparative questions as these must be considered as suggestive only; they cannot be pursued exhaustively for their own sake. Where elements of similarity and difference are seen bound up together, the differences assume greater significance than they would as discrete facts. New meaning attaches to historical or social data that in isolation seem of no importance. And yet this same awareness tells us that thorough-going comparison would lead further and deeper into the labyrinth of each civilization than it is feasible for the non-specialist to follow. (There is a question, indeed whether it is feasible even for the specialist, given the present state of our knowledge). Therefore it seems prudent to avoid involvement in any overall comparison of civilizations, and to put primary emphasis on the articulation of each civilization within itself, while yet placing it side-by-side with others and compelling the student to develop a perspective which embraces both.[4]

At the conference referred to earlier, Professor Arthur Wright, discussing "Chinese History for Undergraduates," acknowledged the value of comparative statements regarding *specific* characteristics of Chinese civilization as both possible and illuminating. "For example, the Chinese monarchy is to be understood (both) in its own particularity *and* by reference to kingship elsewhere."[5] On the other hand, he found that when his students were called on "to compare, for example, Confucian ideas with those of Hobbes or those of Christ in the Bible, his students did not know Hobbes even if their graduation depended on it, and the scantiness of their knowledge of the Bible was truly extraordinary."[6] Professor Hsu countered this "negativism," as he put it, by insisting that:

> If some American students in Oriental studies do not know about Hobbes or the Bible, it is high time for them to do something about it.... I have found that whenever I pointed out to my students the necessity of comparison and confronted them with the poverty of their knowledge about significant thought, theological details, and historical events in their heritage, a majority of them could be galvanized into seriously doing something about it, by shame if not by more lofty motives.[7]

To this it is easy for all of us to say "Amen", but at the same time we cannot help sharing some of Professor Wright's pessimism. It is foolhardy to undertake such a comparison as a class exercise unless one has good reason to believe that most of the students have an adequate knowledge of the two terms of the comparison. Such an exercise in comparativism is, in fact, more likely to achieve its success by revealing the student's ignorance of the two subjects under comparison, than by arriving at a just and rounded judgment. Ulitimately then, whatever benefits derive from the exercise will be in proportion to the specificity and manageability of the comparison. Considering the same issue in relation to our Oriental Humanities course, I have written:

> Comparative analysis of several works can be fruitful only if it deals with specific features or concepts in each work for which the grounds of comparability are well established and explicitly

defined. Comparisons of whole traditions or religions are almost always out of place and have essentially nothing to do with general education. Indeed, exposure to the complexities of different cultural traditions and religious systems should make the student increasingly conscious that such questions, while not insignificant, require a depth of scholarly study and fullness of treatment quite beyond an introductory course. It is not upon their solution that the value of such a course depends, but upon appreciation of the books in and for themselves.[8]

To some, my simultaneous emphasis on the values and limits of the comparative approach in undergraduate course many seem to risk the inducing of a colossal neurosis in the poor undergraduate, as he is caught constantly between intellectual temptation and scholarly frustration. Nor can I deny that some students' papers and themes have a rather wild air about them. Specialists in certain disciplines would no doubt be dismayed at some of the speculations in these papers over problems they are accustomed to handling with much greater precision and finesse. I plead guilty as an accomplice to these crimes, and with deliberate intent, but I hope not the intent, to kill or to stultify the intellectual life of our victim.

The aim of general education courses is forever to discourage pat little answers to big problems. It seeks rather to open up questions which the student should realize are susceptible of further exploration. Most of them he may never have the opportunity to explore himself, he does not expect to specialize in one of the relevant fields. He should be aware of what he does not know as much as of what he does know. He need not know, for instance, what the sociologist knows about such questions, but he should appreciate better what kinds of questions the sociologist can help with and why they are important to him.

For those students who may happen to specialize in Asian studies, the next step, according to the plan outlined previously would be language training and acquisition of a basic scholarly discipline. Here comparative studies would have less of a place, except within the carefully circumscribed limits of a particular methodology. We do not expect, however, that they should be left behind for good, once a student is embarked on specialized study. As the climax of undergraduate training in the senior year, students who have achieved some competence in both an Asian language and scholarly discipline, are brought together in seminars which deal on a cross-cultural basis with materials appropriate to their language and discipline.

During our first experimental year with this program, we have offered four inter-departmental seminars. The first of these, a social science seminar, examined the conceptions of Asian civilization held by twenty-four social and political thinkers in the Western tradition from Plato and Aristotle to Hegel Marx and Weber. It was conducted by three regular teachers of the Oriental Civilizations staff, with Professor Karl Wittfogel as a guest professor from the University of Washington. The second social science seminar focused on problems in the modernization of India, China, and Japan. Leading specialists from the Anthropology, Sociology, History, Government, and Economics Departments joined members of the Oriental Studies Committee in this group, which included students from a similar variety of disciplinary and area backgrounds.

A humanities seminar, dealing with the classical poetry of India, China, and Japan, was conducted by Professor Burton Watson of the Department of Chinese and Japanese and Professor Barry Ulanov of the English Department of Barnard College. They were joined by other members of the Oriental Studies Committee in conducting another seminar for students in the humanities dealing with the development of fiction in modern India, China, and Japan.

There were good practical reasons for organizing these seminars on an inter-departmental basis, since it is difficult to find enough college students concentrating in the same area and discipline to populate such special courses. Nevertheless, the comparative approach adopted in these seminars was fully justified intellectually, according to the unanimous judgment of the rather large number of instructors drawn from different departments. Even if there were a population exploison in this field, those in charge would not be inclined to abandon the comparative approach for a more specialized one. Apparently, then, the rationale and method of the general education courses has validity even on the more advanced level.

Equal parts of temptation and frustration in handling comparative problems in the introductory courses seem not to have done irreparable damage to our college students. The comparative appropriately modified and adjusted to the proper level of advancement, seems to have a secure place in the sequence of Asian studies.

Notes

1. Wm. Theodore De Bary, "Education for a World Community," in *Liberal Education*, Vol. 1. No. 4, December 1964.

2. *Ibid.*, p. 452.

3. Francis L.K. Hsu, "On behalf of Comparative Civilization Through Intellectual Cooperation Between Disciplines,", in Wm. Theodore de Bary, *Approaches to Asian Civilizations*. 1964, pp. 210-12

4. Wm. Theodore de Bary, *Approaches to Asian Civilizations*, pp. xv, xvi.

5. Arthur Wright, "Chinese History for the Undergraduates," in *ibid.*, pp. 11 and 12.

6. As quoted by Hsu, *op. cit.*, pp. 211-12.

7. Idem.

8. Wm. Theodore de Bary and Ainslie T. Embree. ed., *A Guide to Oriental Classics*, 1964, p. 8.

A Conceptual Review of Area and Comparative Studies : Some Initial Reflections[1]

C.K. YANG*

Among the intellectual currents in the Western world during the past two and a half decades of wartime and postwar setting, has been the rise of area studies and somewhat later, comparative studies in social sciences and humanities. Such currents represent self-conscious expressions of a rapidly emerging world community. Now that these studies have lost much of their sense of novelty, the development seems to have lost some of its initial momentum. Since the related development of comparative studies has fully come into its own, it may be helpful to undertake a conceptual review of the two intellectual currents for the benefit of the cross-cultural approach to the social sciences. This review encompasses problems of both research and training, as seen through the biases of a sociologist.

The academic genesis of "area" studies can be traced back quite far—for example, by anthropologists to tribal and community studies in Africa, in the Pacific islands, and, in Latin America. But are a studies as we know them in university curricula and in research programs in the 1940's and 1950's rode to academic prominence mainly as a response to practical wartime and postwar needs for "area" information and specialists, and not essentially as the product of an evolutionary process of scientific growth and academic development.

This origin from "practical needs" produced certain theoretical weaknesses in area studies. Thus there is the unsettled problem of defining an "area" by natural, cultural. ethnic, political, economic, or other criteria. Should European and Asiatic Russia, for example, be treated as a single area? Then follows the matter of defining "area" study" for theoretical purposes. From a theoretical viewpoint, area studies may be said to be an attempt at synthesis or integration of multidisciplinary specialized knowledge about an area, however the latter is defined, and the scientific objective of this attempt is the understanding of an area as a functioning socio-cultural whole. As I understand it, this is, by and large, the operational definition used by "area specialists" particularly anthropologists.

The next question is how has such an attempt been carried out in research and teaching over the past two and a half decades? To answer the question, let us keep in mind that the definition contains

---

*C. K. Yang is a Professor of Sociology at the University of Pittsburgh. He is the author of *Chinese Communist : Society Family and Village, Religion in Chinese Society*, and other studies of Chinese society.

two separate components : specialized knowledge of certain aspects of an area developed by the disciplines (anthropology, sociology, economics, political science), and the integration or synthesis of these diverse fields of knowledge into a functioning system of interdependent parts.

Thus far, from the many "area" programs has come some progress in empircal knowledge of individual aspects of an area, as developed by separate disciplines. But it is an open question whether such knowledge should be labeled area knowledge or disciplinary knowledge (for example in philosophy, literature, sociology, or economics on an area like China). The integration of this knowledge into a socio-cultural whole remains a serious question for the most part. In short, area studies as such has advanced few conceptual propositions on the theoretical nature of individual areas or on areas as large generalized units of human existence. In actual operation—with rare exceptions, such as the results from the Russian Research Center of Harvard—successful studies of an "area" have been limited to small individual communities or tribes. For more extensive areas like nations and regions, the magnitude and complexity of the task has prevented significant progress in intergration of diverse specialized knowledge as interdependent parts of a total system.

For illustration of this point, let us take the case of China as an area. In the past quarter of a century, the understanding of China has indeed been advanced by publication of many outstanding volumes on special aspects of Chinese culture and society (history, philosophy, anthropology, sociology, political science). But what outstanding volume can we cite to represent integration or synthesis of these specialized contributions into a socio-cultural whole? For this purpose we may immediately think of such monumental works by individual scholars as *The Chinese, Their History and Culture* by K. S. Latourrette[2] or such a collective undertaking as H. F. MacNair's *China*[3] which was the forerunner for many similar edited volumes. To be sure, all these volumes have enhanced the understanding of the China area. But should we regard them as summaries of separate compartments of specialized knowledge about China, or should we regard them as integrated scientific propositions on China as a socio-cultural whole built of diverse but interdependent parts? The individual chapters represent knowledge of different disciplines, but are they explicitly interpreted as interdependent parts and what has been the generalized and integrated nature of the "whole"?

If the present state of development has brought but little progress in theoretical knowledge of areas as integrated entities, can we assign much scientific meaning to such area study terms as Sinology and Indology? Is a China area specialist a jack of all trades about China, or does he possess certain theoretical skills for dealing with China as an integrated comprehensive whole? If, on the other hand, a scientifically sound scholar is one who specializes in certain aspects of an area, should he be designated an area specialist or a scholar in the respective discipline, such as an economist on China?

In a scientific sense, the ultimate goal of area studies is not the understanding of areas as special individual cases, but the development of concepts and theories which can be applied to all areas—that is, scientific knowledge of universal validity. In the present state of knowledge, the way toward this goal may not be the study of areas—at least large, complex areas—as integrated socio-cultural wholes.

As noted previously, successful integration of diverse and specialized knowledge for large and complex areas is rare; even if successfully achieved, what holds for one area may not be applicable for another. No concept or theory can be regarded as applicable to two or more areas without adequate comparative study of those areas. And comparison of two or more large and complex areas in their totality, either in concrete or in abstract patterns, is presently difficult if not impossible. At this stage, what can be profitably compared, therefore, are similar parts of two or more areas, such as the family systems of two or more cultural areas. Such studies can be more adequately subsumed under the designation of comparative study, and not area study, for their chief concern is not the area, but the elements comprising an area.

Comparative study generally involves attempts to discover similarities or differences between two or more units of social facts of the same category in separate social systems, with the eventual objective of formulating concepts and theories of universal validity. Comparative study, it is true, need not always involve a comparison of the same category of facts from two or more societies. The test of a Western-based concept or theoretical scheme against non-Western facts of a relevant category should also constitute comparative study, because Western-based concepts or theories embody Western facts, though in generalized and not in concrete form. As present-day social science theories are almost exclusively based on Western facts, the test of theoretical propositions against non-Western facts should constitute comparative study. Such tests would tend to universalize the validity of Western-based social science theory. Conversely, a study can be regarded as comparative if it tests a theoretical scheme derived from, say, Chinese facts on the analysis of Western life.

Following this broadened definition, many scientific works on non-Western societies, based on Western concepts or frames of reference, would fall under the heading of comparative study. On the other hand, the number of comparative studies would be relatively small if we were confined to the strict definiton of point-for-point comparison of facts of the same category between two or more societies.

Comparative study differs from area study in two important respects. First, while area study tends to concentrate on one area, comparative study is concerned with cross-area (or cross-cultural) analysis. Second, area study, at least in practice if not in theory, inclines toward concrete facts more than conceptualized problems and abstract generalizations, while comparative study has the opposite interest. Since no two facts or phenomena are completely alike in all concrete details they cannot be compared in the concrete. It follows that comparative study, by its nature, must be based on conceptualized problems and abstract generalizations, foumulated for studying certain aspects of an entity.

In studying the status advancement of humble men to respectability, for example, a concrete description of two particular individuals in two separate areas or societies and a factual account of their status advancement would not be regarded as a comparative study. A comparative study would formulate the conceptual problem of social status mobility and proceed to compare the generalized types of people, types of status, and types of channels and procedures involved in achieving the mobility, as well as the degree of mobility achieved.

There could be many possible ways of classifying comparative studies. One way could be to follow the sociological classification by structure, function, and process. This method may be explained by the several illustrations which follow.

Structurally, two or more socio-cultural systems can be compared with respect to certain of their respective subsystem component characteristics. Robert Redfield's *Peasant Society and Culture* is an excellent example.[4] Treating peasants as a component of complex society, Redfield tried to find universal characteristics of peasant life and personality in all complex societies. This is the basis for his remark that an American farmer would understand a Chinese peasant more readily than he would a Wall Street businessman.

From the peasant life he observed, Redfield abstracted certain variables which appeared significant to him as factors in the organized existence of peasantry and constructed a subsystem model, the peasant society. Comparison can be made between different peasant societies by studying the similarities and differences of these variables. Such comparison is based on an abstract system of variables oriented toward a problem, not on detailed concrete facts.

In addition to Redfield's scheme, we can make up many other analytic designs for the comparative study of peasant communities in an effort to discover universal characteristics of peasant life in complex societies. Thus, we can study comparatively, the ramifying effects of the seemingly universal variables of low spatial mobility, the repetitive organic cycle of crops and husbandry, the single-industry base, the family farm and self-sufficient farming, and the lack of flexibility or expansibility of agricultural land as the chief production factor.

From such variables we can study the effects on patterns of peasant life, such as low socio-economic differentiation and its corollary of high importance of diffuse organizations like the multifunctional kinship system, internal cohesion but external isolation of village life, low population mobility, low occupational mobility, low rate of class mobility, and cycles of land ownership concentration and dispersion which underlie repetitive socio-political crises. These variables and their resulting characteristics in the life of peasant communities have been observed in many societies, and they can be used for the construction of schemes of comparative study of peasant villages.

Some elaboration may serve to clarify this analytic scheme. A peasant village is based on peasant farming characterised by, among other things, the self-sufficient family farm. This leads to the major trait of the peasant village—an *earthbound* life.[5] Farm land is not mobile like machinery or business, the physical locations of which can be changed. The ownership of a peasant farm, furthermore, is relatively immobile. Peasant villages appear to discriminate, often forbid, sale of land to outsiders and to impose other restrictions on land transaction. The self-sufficient family farm, generally hand-operated and small in size, yields little surplus for the purchase of another farm in a new location.

As the peasant cannot easily liquidate his farm (assuming he owns the land) and move to another village, he is tied down to the soil in the same village, usually for generations. Multiplying its members on the same spot for a long period, with a restriction against outsiders moving in, the peasant village develops such characteristics as population immobility, insulation from the outside world, conservatism (partly because of lack of outside stimulation), the basic importance of the family as a farming organization, the extended family and the clan as the dominant integrating structures for the village community, and a high degree of intra-village solidarity based on population immobility and on kinship ties in case of single-surname villages.

Next to earthbound immobility as a significant trait of the peasant village is the anture of the village's sustenance base—peasant farming as the single dominant industry and preoccupation with the simple organic cycle of crops and husbandry. (Major development of rural supplementary industries may alter the picture a bit, but it does not distort the outline.) This leads toward the development of a low degree of division of labor in the economic sphere and lack of structural differentiation in the social system. There is a minimum specialization of tasks both in the individual's activities and in the functions of organizations. Dominating the village life are such highly diffuse organizations as the family and the clan which perform a multiplicity of functions from economic production to spiritual worship, and which meet the comprehensive needs of the individual from cradle to grave.

Hence, in a peasant village there are very few organizations besides kin groups and the family farm, and rare are organizations whose sole task is to produce a single product or to perform a single service. If specialization and diversity are basic conditions for development of complex communities of the urban type, there is no breeding ground for them in the one-industry economy and in the confinement to the fixed organic cycle (as contrasted with the infinite possibility of diversification in artificial products of urban industry and commerce). By the very nature of its economy, the peasant village finds it difficult, if not impossible, to advance beyond a simple structural level.

The self-sufficient family farm, as a dominant factor in the single-industry base and and in insulating the village from the outside world, has multiple consequences for the life of the peasantry. There is minimal occupational mobility as a means of adjustment of the employable population to economic resources and as a channel of advancement in socio-economic status. Social class mobility is slow as a consequence of these factors, augmented by effects from the land tenancy situation and low per-capita productivity of the family farm, which yields little surplus or saving for status improvement. A peasant family frequently remains in the same class status for generations. The occasional significant uplift of status represents achievement by emigrants in the outside world, through industry, commerce, or officialdom, rather than successful operation within the village economy. The lack of class mobility generates tension and conflict and obstructs the flow of talented and ambitious elements from lower strata into village leadership.

Related to class mobility is the vital matter of land ownership and tenancy in the freehold and open class system. It appears that there is a rather long-term cycle of concentration and dispersion of land ownership related to the alternation between tranquility and upheaval of the socio-political order. The supply of agricultural land within the village boundary is rather inflexible, as land reclamation from whatever source is extremely slow. Periodic concentration of land ownership in the hands of the minority forces the majority into tenancy and eventually reduces peasant farming below the subsistence level where minimum health and security for the family cannot be maintained. Any extensive development of this condition would create the classical background for peasant uprisings, explosive socio-political crises and, eventually, dispersion of land ownership as a means of restoring the peasant family farm to a profitable level.

This generalised characterization of the peasant village and peasant life, based largely on examination of Chinese cases, constitutes a possible first step in comparative study of peasant societies, as it poses conceptual problems for discovering universal features of peasant villages in other cultures. Thus we may ask whether all peasant villages are characterized by earth-bound immobility of their populations, dominance of the self-sufficient family form and the kinship system, the prevalence of diffuse organizations and particularistic relations, a high degree of intra-village solidarity and insularity from the outside world, a low degree of socio-economic differentiation low class mobility, and a cyclical process of concentration and dispersion of land ownership and its socio-political consequences.

A counterpart to comparative study of peasant communities is that of urban communities. Works on modern urban communities are limited to cross-national comparisons within the industrial culture, resulting mainly in intra-cultural typologies. But such works as Gideon Sjoberg's *The Preindustrial City*[6] represent extensive comparative studies of urban communities of many diverse cultures. Cities had long been vital centers of organized activities in all known preindustrial complex societies, and this lends importance to comparative study of pre-industrial urban communities. Many research designs can be developed from such generalized problems as size, typology, ecological patterns, class structure and mobility, and the nature of organizational systems.

To take the first of the problems cited, there is the illustrative problem of an international definition for the city in terms of population size. UNESCO for example, has struggled with this question. Should the minimum population of an urban place be 500, 2,000, 5,000, or still another figure? As the size of a community in which urban characteristics develop varies according to the type of socio-economic milieu, it may be necessary to set a classification of minimum sizes in relation to the nature of their respective societies, instead of a single size-standard of urban community for all nations with their widely varying types of socio-economic development. But cross-cultural case analyses and comparisons are needed in order to establish classified minimum size-standards of urban places for different societies or nations. There is also need for a unified list of variables representing urban characteristics (e.g., a majority engaged in non-agricultural employment) and the minimum size of communities in which these develop. Up to now, we still lack a systematic cross-cultural study of the correlation between size and urban traits.

The rank-size order of the system of cities is another relevant point for comparative study. The rank size order as developed in the United States contains a system of cities in which the size of urban places descends by 50 per cent from one rank to the next (1,000,000, 500,000 etc.). This rank-size order serves to spread urbanization deep into the countryside in the Western industrialized nations. But we do not have comparative information on rank-size order of urban places in non-industrial societies, where there may be much wider gaps between size-ranks (dropping from 1,000,000 to 100,000 for example) and where urban traits may be restricted to a few big cities without any significant penetration into the countryside. The later pattern seems to characterize the Chinese case from general observation, but careful statistical analysis may lead to a different conclusion.

Comparative study of urban typology is significant for an adequate understanding of various types of societies, as the presence or absence of some types of urban centers may indicate certain characteristics for the social system. A case in point might be the familiar claim that preindustrial societies have no truly economic cities but only centers of political power and administration where economic development is for the consumption of those holding power and not for the benefit of other classes or the surrounding regions. The significance of an "economic city" is that it serves as a point of concentration and distribution of commodities, thus providing the integrating link for regional and inter-regional economic systems and the socio-economic environment for the development of a business class possessing wealth and influence. On this assumption, the absence of "economic cities" in a society would mean the corresponding absence of regional and inter-regional economies to any degree and the lack of a business class of any consequence.

An examination of the nature of cities in such preindustrial cultures as the Chinese or the Japanese suggests, however, the presence of "economic" factors serving as regional and inter-regional integrators and producing commodities not only for the politically powerful, but also for a significant business class in the cities as well as for consumers in the surrounding countryside. One point is quite definite. At least in preindustrial China, there has been considerable development of a regional and inter-regional economy; and this could not take place without "economic cities" as integrators. Equally definite is the presence of an economically significant, business class in Chinese cities, and this class has to be served by the city economy. But it will take careful cross-cultural study to establish definitely the presence or absence of the so-called "economic cities" in pre-industrial cultures.

Comparative study of urban communities could further take up the subject of ecological patterns. It would examine such problems as the homogeneous craft areas, the mixing of business and residence quarters, the highly organized neighborhood units and the distribution of slums (concentration in the suburbs and irregular distribution within the city, instead of blighted areas near the business center as in the case of expanding American cities). There is also the problem of class structure and mobility—the relative position of the business class as a contribution from the urban community to the national stratification order, and the function of the city in facilitating class status mobility. For instance, medieval European cities offered serfs political freedom while Chinese cities helped peasants with business opportunities as a means of status improvement. There is finally the problem of organizational patterns which enabled cities throughout history in different cultures to play the consistent role of being the staging center for the large-scale collective activities—as in bureaucracies, guilds, territorial groups, and "interest" organizations, which expanded the boundaries of organized action beyond the narrow confinement of kinship ties.

Without lengthy elaboration, we may enumerate further areas for comparative study. Feudalism as a political community is another subject of significance in need of comparative treatment. We find similar forms of political communities in both European and Asian histories, and their limited size and relative structural simplicity make it possible to devise systematic comparisons for discovering their more precise similarities and differences as an alternative to the loose speculation which seems to have characterized discussion of this subject so far. Comparative study of this topic would contribute toward resolution of the controversy of unilinear versus multi-linear evolution of human society.

The above cases concern comparative study of community subsystems of complex societies. In addition, we can consider comparative study of institutional subsystems as structural components of societies. In this category there are large numbers of outstanding works to serve as examples.

A monumental forerunner is, of course, Max Weber's series on comparative study of religions in Europe, Israel, India, and China, a task initially motivated by his attempt to answer the question of why industrialism developed in Europe but not in other societies.[7] Beyond Weber's original scope, comparative study of religions remains a vital task for the development of concepts and theories that can successfully explain religious phenomena and trends cross-culturally—for example, the Buddhist movement in contemporary Vietnam.

Another instance of comparative study of institutions is the recent interest in comparative bureaucracy. This, too, received significant stimulus from Max Weber's pioneering work, which not only set the instrument of the "ideal type" of modern Western bureaucracy but also formulated typologies of pre-modern bureaucracies in other societies. S.N. Eisenstadt's recent *Political Systems of Empires*[8] compared 27 historical societies and worked out "universal" conditions for the development of bureaucracy. Fred Riggs compared several contemporary bureaucracies in Western and non-Western cultures in order to test Weber's "ideal type" definition of bureaucracy in terms of identifying traits and components. I have also tested Weber's model against traditional Chinese bureaucratic behavior as a means of establishing a typology which will fit the Chinese case and meanwhile add to the cross-cultural validity of current theories of bureaucracy. This subject of comparative study has added interest in the modern world due to the increasing bureaucratization of modern social organization.

An old favorite of comparative institutional study concerns the family and the wider kinship system. The history of such studies is long, and the accumulated literature is considerable, mainly in the fields of anthropology and sociology.[9] This subject is of vital interest in view of the transformation of the so-called non-Western world, where the pivotal institution of family is undergoing an alteration which is not yet consistently explainable by existing (Western-based) concepts and theories on the structure and change of the family institution. Even in the modern community of New York, the existence of differential rates of juvenile delinquency in such ethnic groups as the Italian and the Chinese has led to comparative study of the respective family systems as a possible causal factor.

We may say that comparative studies have been conducted in all institutional spheres of societies cross-culturally. One more structural component of socio-cultural systems which has significance for the field of comparative study should be noted—the stratification order.

Social stratification or the class system is universal among complex societies, but there is not yet any theoretical scheme universally applicable to its cross-cultural analysis despite convergence of interests from the disciplines. The easier part of the subject-matter concerns the relative rates of class mobility in different societies—for example, the percentage of commoners rising to the gentry stratum in imperial China.[10] So long as variables are properly defined, statistical figures can be compared. But comparative analysis of the causes of the differential rates—for instance, status values and the elite demand theory—and of pattern variations in stratification structure would be much more difficult. These involve searching for a cross-culturally applicable group of variables and a design suitable for comparison.

Theoretically, even the basic matter of strata division remains unsettled on a cross-cultural basis.[11] Extensive comparative study is necessary to yield a cross-culturally applicable theoretical scheme as a means of adequately understanding the structure and operation of the stratification order. This task takes on practical current interest in this age of revolutions, since the alteration of the social class system is constantly a major target for revolutions. Similarly important for the present-day revolutionary world is the comparative study of value systems and ideologies, which supply the motivation and directionality to trends of changing social structures, but there is no space for its consideration here.

In addition to the structural components of socio-cultural wholes, as discussed above, there is the comparative study of functions of the structural components. This is actually inseparable from any thorough analysis of social structural-functional viewpoint. It is difficult to think of studying a structural component or system without inquiring into its functions. For instance, comparing the size and structure of the extended family in traditional China with those of the Western nuclear family, we cannot escape from studying their similarities and differences in functions.

Such comparative knowledge in functions of two divergent family systems helps in the interpretation of similarities or differences in their structure. It may also yield indicators of trends of change from one system to another. Thus, the reduction of family functions in modern China presages a trend toward the Western nuclear family, and the Communist removal of the production function from the family will inevitably bring an alteration in the status structure within the family. But it would take extensive inter-cultural comparisons to establish evidence for such hypotheses.

There is, finally, the subject of comparative study of social processes. This is an extensive and complex field, and only random examples can be discussed here. One instance is the perennial effort to discover the universal stages or time sequence of social development. But any theoretical development in this direction would require extensive and rigorous cross-cultural comparison before any universal validity can be established. Thus, the Marxist theory falters when agrarian Russia and China and not the industrial West went Communist and when American capitalism changed its nineteenth-century nature instead of collapsing under a revolution.

Among the most tested sociological theories of social change is that of "cultural lag", which postulates that cultural institutions constantly lag behind technology in the differential rates of change. But this exclusively Western-based theory, when applied to the modern non-Western world, fails the test of empirical evidence. The non-Western world, for a century, has been desperately altering the cultural institutions (from values to government and education) in order to induce technological change. Thus, cultural institutions changed first and technology changed later, if at all. The case is one of "technological lag", not "cultural lag". To gain cross-cultural validity, the theory of "cultural lag" needs comparative study to give it the needed qualifying conditions and refinement, and social change initiated by cultural diffusion from outside (the exogenic type) perhaps needs a very different theory as an explanation.

The whole range of current studies on industrialization and modernization of the non-Western world, including the so-called institution-building research, would find it almost impossible to achieve sound development without the techniques and approach of comparative study. Why did Japan succeed and pre-Communist China fail at industrialization, and what lessons does this comparison hold for developing countries in other parts of Asia and Africa ? Why did a new organization financed by American foreign aid prove viable in one country but evaporate rapidly in other countries as soon as American aid was withdrawn ? Why was there a differential reaction from diverse socio-cultural environments ? Comparative study holds an important key to such problems.

This rapidly unifying world demands the service of a universally valid body of theoretical knowledge in the social sciences so that it can better understand a common set of social and technological forces which are subjecting the entire world to their impact. It is perhaps the discipline-based comparative study, and not so much the integrative area study, that will meet this need.

Notes

1. These notes, containing all of the inadequacies and other characteristics of initial reflections on a complex subject, have been put down in writing here only as a response to Professor Chan's call for early submission of a paper growing out of my participation in the Dartmouth conference on Asian studies and comparative approaches.

2. 1946.

3. 1946.

4. 1956.

5. *See* Introduction in H. T. Fei and Chih-i Chang *Earthbound China* : *A Study of Rural Economy in Yunan*, 1949.

6. Gideon Sjoberg, *The Preindustrial City* : *Past and Present,* 1965.

7. Max Weber, *The Religion of China* : *Confucianism and Taoism,* tr, and ed. by Hans, H. Gerth, 1951,

8. S. N, Eisenstadt, *Political Systems of Empires,* 1962.

9. For instance, George Peter Murdoch, *Social Structure*, 1949.

10. Chung-li Chang, *The Chinese Gentry* : *Studies on their Role in Nineteenth Century Chinese Society 1955.* and Ping-ti Ho, *Studies on the Population of China, 1368-1953,* 1959.

11. William Lloyd Warner, *Yankee City,* 1963.

A Note on the Foreign Area Materials Center

The State Education Department is actively concerned with strengthening opportunities and resources for the study of foreign areas in the schools, colleges, and universities of New York. Emphasis is being placed on the peoples, cultures, and contemporary institutions of those areas traditionally neglected in American education—namely, Asia, Africa, Latin America, Russia, and Eastern Europe.

Recent efforts of the Department in foreign area studies include faculty fellowships, summer faculty seminars, programs of independent readings ; encouragement of faculty research : programs of independent reading and seminar discussion, summer institutes, and other opportunities for secondary school teachers ; consultant services to schools, colleges, and universities in developing foreign area studies ; and experimental programs in the study of critical languages in schools and colleges, summer field work overseas for students and teachers, and the like. Surveys of museum and library resources on foreign areas have also been been undertaken in an attempt to relate these resources more effectively to programs of study in schools and colleges.

As a further extension of these efforts to strengthen foreign areas studies, the State Education Department established in December 1963, the Foreign Area Materials Center. The Center, which is located in New York City, is concerned with the development of materials useful in teaching about foreign area, mainly at the undergraduate level.

Types of materials which have been produced or are in preparation include color slides in South Asian studies, reproductions of museum materials from India, reviews of documentary films on foreign areas, and bibliographies of paperback books, records, and the like. The Center provides liaison with publishers and other organizations producing materials useful in undergraduate instruction and is particularly concerned with out-of-print books and other needs of college libraries. These activities are being supported by grants from foundation sources and the United States government.

The Center also distributes various types af syllabi and reprints, bibliographies, and similar materials to college faculty members offering courses related to the Center's main areas of interest—Asia, Africa, Latin America, Russia, and Eastern Europe. A list of materials is available on request.

The Foreign Area Materials Center is under the direction of Ward Morehouse, Director, and Don Peretz, Assistant Director, Center for International Programs and Services. The Manager of the Center in New York City is Miss Edith Ehrman.

Correspondence regarding any of the activities mentioned above and requests for materials should be directed to the Foreign Area Materials Center (33 West 42nd Street, New York, N.Y. 10036). Correspondence concerning other aspects of the Department's programs in foreign area studies should be sent to the Director, Center for International Programs and Services, University of the State of New York, State Education Department, Albany, N.Y. 12224.

Some Publications of the Foreign Area Materials Center

Occasional Publications Series

Ward Morehouse, Editor, Foreign Area Studies and the College Library. 1964, (FAMC Occasional Publication No.1.). $ 1.00,

L. A. Peter Gosling, Maps, Atlases and Gazetteers for Asian Studies : A Critical Guide, 1965. (FAMC Occasional Publicacation No. 2) $ 1.00.

Patrick Wilson, Science in South Asia, Past & Present : A Preliminary Bibliography, 1966. (FAMC Occasional Publication No. 3) $ 2.00.

Ward Morehouse, editor, The Comparative Approach in Area Studies and the Disciplines : Problems of Teaching and Research on Asia, 1966. (FAMC Occasional Publication No. 4) $ 2.00.

Checklists of Paperbound Books

David H. Andrews, compiler, and T.J. Hillman, Editor, Latin America : A Bibliography of Paperback books, 1964. 35c. each from Government Printing Office, Washington, D.C. 10420.

Cynthia T. Morehouse, compiler, Paperbound Books on Asia, 1966, $ 1.00.

Paul Rosenblum, compiler, Checklist of Paperbound Books on Africa, 1965. 35c.

Sherman D. Spector and Lyman Legters, compilers, Checklist of Paperbound Books on Russia and East Europe, 1969. 80.

Other Materials

Edith Ehrman, editor, Guide to Asian Studies in Undergraduate Education, 1964. 25c.

A number of syllabi, course outlines and teaching notes, bibliographies, and other materials are also available from the Foreign Area Materials Center. A list of these materials will be sent on request.

Minimum order for priced publications, $ 1.00; all orders must be prepaid. Checks should be drawn to the University of the State of New York.

Foreign Area Materials Center, University of the State of New York, State Education Department, 33 West 42nd Street, New York, N.Y. 10036.

APPENDIX

Conference on Asian Studies and Comparative Approaches

Comparative Studies Center
Dartmouth College
September 13-17, 1965

PROGRAMME

Chairman: Lyman H. Legters, Chief of Institutional Assistance Section, Division of Foreign Studies, U.S. Office of Education

Paper: Joseph Campbell, "Comparative Mythology as an Introduction to Cross-Cultural Studies"

Chairman: Norman A. Doenges, Associate Dean and Chairman of the Division of the Humanities, Dartmouth College

Paper: George L. Anderson, "Comparative Literature Studies, Critical and Historical: Some Porsibilities and Some Limits"

Chairman: Robert E. Huke, Associate Professor of Geography, Dartmouth College

Paper: Edward S. Jurji, "Islamic Setting in Comparative Religion"

Chairman: Henry C. Fenn, Visiting Professor of Chinese, Dartmouth College

Paper: Wm. Theodore de Bary, "Comparative Studies in Undergraduate Education"

Chairman: Donald Bartlett, Professor of Japanese Studies and Chairman of the Department of Biography, Dartmouth College

Paper: Donald H. Shively, "Approaches in the Study of Japan"

Chairman: Colin D. Campbell, Chairman, of the Department of Economics, Dartmouth College

Paper: Ernest P, Young, "The Soldier and Nationalism: Military Modernization in Early Twentieth Century China"

Chairman: Allen McCormick, Chairman of the Department of German, Dartmouth College

Paper: Milton Singer "On Comparative Study of Civilizations"

Chairman: Matthew I. Wiencke, Chairman of the Department of Classic, Dartmouth College

Paper: Howard L. Erdman, "Indian Conservatism and Comparative Politics"

Chairman: William Smith, Associate Dean and Chairman of the Division of Social Sciences, Dartmouth College

Paper: Charles B. McLane, "Comparative Study and the Area Specialist"

Chairman: James F. Hornig, Associate Dean and Chairman of the Division of Sciences, Dartmouth College

Paper: C. K. Yang, "A Conceptual Review of Area and Comparative Studies"

PARTICIPANTS

Anderson, George L., Modern Language Association (comparative literature)

Bartlett Donald, Dartmouth College (Japanese civilization)

Campbell, Joseph, Sarah Lawrence College (comparative mythology)

Chan, Wing-tsit, Dartmouth College (Chinese philosophy)

Chu, Yu-kuang, Skidmore College (Asian civilizations; education)

Crane Robert I., Duke University (India; history)

de Bary, Wm. Theodore., Columbia University (China ; Japan: Neo-Confucianism)

Duggan, Timothy J., Dartmouth College (philosophy)

Ehrmann, Henry W., Dartmouth College (government)

Feldmesser, Robert A, Dartmouth College (sociology)

Goodwin, Delmar, Hanover High School (Africa and Middle East)

Gramlich, Francis W., Dartmouth College (philosophy)

Hines, Lawrence, Dartmouth College (economics)

Jensen, Arthur E., Dartmouth College (English literature)

Jurji, Edward L., Princeton Theological Seminary (Islam)

Legters, Lyman H., U.S. Office of Education (East Europe and Russia; history)

Little, George T., University of Vermont (China; Western Pacfic law)

McLane, Charles B., Dartmouth College (Asia; international relations)

Michael, Franz, University of Washington (China; modern history)

Morehouse, Ward, University of the State of New York (India; political science)

Morton, Louis, Dartmouth College (history)

Raju, P. T., College of Wooster (India; comparative philosophy)

Reed, Howard, Education and World Affairs (Near East; history, Islamic and intercultural studies)

Roberts, F. David, Dartmouth College (history)

Sakamaki, Shunzo, University of Hawaii (Japan; history)

Schultz, Harry T., Dartmouth College (English literature)

Shively, Donald H., Harvard University (Japan; history)

Singer, Milton, University of Chicago (India: anthropology)

Vance, Thomas H., Dartmouth College (English literature)

Welbon, Guy Richard, University of Rochester (India; Sanskrit and Pali)

Williams, Henry B., Dartmouth College (Japan; drama)

Williams, Lea E., Brown University (Southeast Asia; political science)

Yang, C. K., Universities of Pittsburgh and Hawaii (China; sociology)

Young, Ernest P., Dartmouth College (East Asia; history)